THE
LANGUAGE
GOD TALKS

THE
LANGUAGE
GOD TALKS

On Science and Religion

HERMAN WOUK

Little, Brown and Company
New York   Boston   London

Little, Brown and Company
Hachette Book Group
237 Park Avenue, New York, NY 10017
www.hachettebookgroup.com

First Edition: April 2010

Little, Brown and Company is a division of Hachette Book Group, Inc. The Little, Brown name and logo are trademarks of Hachette Book Group, Inc.

Library of Congress Cataloging-in-Publication Data
Wouk, Herman.
    The language God talks : on science and religion / Herman Wouk.—1st ed.
        p. cm.
    ISBN 978-0-316-07845-0
    1. Religion and science.   I. Title.
    BL240.3.W68 2010
    201'.65—dc22   2009038522

10 9 8 7 6 5 4 3 2 1

RRD-IN

Book design by Renato Stanisic

Printed in the United States of America

To the memory of our fathers

ABRAHAM ISAAC WOUK
MELVILLE FEYNMAN

*who emigrated from Minsk
and gave us our lives in America*

It doesn't seem to me that this fantastically marvelous universe, this tremendous range of time and space and different kinds of animals, and all the different planets, and all these atoms with all their motions, and so on, all this complicated thing can merely be a stage so that God can watch human beings struggle for good and evil— which is the view that religion has. The stage is too big for the drama.

—RICHARD FEYNMAN

Remember, Herman Wouk, we are storytellers. Stories, pictures, people! No thoughts!

—S. Y. AGNON

THE
LANGUAGE
GOD TALKS

CHAPTER ONE

The Language God Talks

More years ago than I care to reckon up, I met Richard Feynman. I was then out to write a sort of *War and Peace* of World War II, and early on in the moonstruck enterprise I realized that if I were at all serious about it, I had to learn something right away about the atomic bomb. Tolstoy could not consult Kutuzov, the general who drove Napoleon out of Russia, because the canny old one-eyed field marshal was long since dead; but when I started to work on my unlikely notion nearly all the men who had created the bomb were alive, and several of them were at the California Institute of Technology, including Feynman. President Truman, who had been an artilleryman in World War I, said of the bomb, "It was a bigger piece of artillery, so I used it," a striking remark which shows up in my *War and Remembrance* but surely something less than the whole story. So I went to Caltech to talk to those who knew the whole story.

This may seem monstrously pushy, and no doubt it was.

Like many novelists I have spun my books out of my own experiences when I could, but in attempting work far outside my own relatively jog-trot existence I have had to pick other men's brains. My World War II service, three years on destroyer-minesweepers in the Pacific, gave me the substance of *The Caine Mutiny,* but taught me nothing at all about the world storm that had swept me from Manhattan to the South Pacific like a driven leaf. When the bomb fell on Hiroshima my ship was a bobbing speck on picket duty in the rough waters off Okinawa, and we had just survived a kamikaze attack unscathed; so I joined heartily in the merriment aboard ship, very glad that I had survived the war and would soon go back to my free civilian life and marry my sweetheart. As to the larger issues of dropping a whacking new bomb made of uranium on a Japanese city, I was innocent and indifferent. The radio said that our scientists had "harnessed the power of the Sun," and that was quite enough for me and for all of us aboard that old four-piper, halfway around the world from home.

The Caltech scientists received me cordially, and talked freely about their adventures in working on the bomb. I remember one physicist telling me, for instance, how he drove to the Trinity test site in New Mexico with the dread plutonium core in the back seat of his car. But to a man, one after another, they warned me so earnestly not to try to see Richard Feynman, that I began to think of him as a human plutonium core. However, I had nothing to lose so I did try, and somehow I found myself in his office, talking to a lean guy in white shirtsleeves, with long hair and a sharply humorous countenance calling to mind a bust of Voltaire. It didn't go well at first. "You know," he said, as I groped to explain my purpose, "while you're talking, you're not learning anything." So I blurted out baldly, any old way, my vision of a fiction work throwing a rope around the whole global war. As I spoke an enigmatic look came over that strong face, something like remote tolerant amusement. "Well, that's the sort of thing genius reaches out for," he said, and he took over the conversation.

In swift strokes Feynman brought the entire Manhattan Project to life, the excitement and the perils alike, mentioning that once in a laboratory corridor he passed uranium materials stacked so carelessly that a chain reaction was within a whisker of going off. His main point was that the whole enterprise was gigantically messy, and that the atomic bomb was by no means at a frontier of science. He put it so: "It wasn't a lion hunt, it was a rabbit shoot." There was no Nobel Prize, that is to say, in the concept or the calculations; it was just a challenge, if a huge one, to audacious innovative technology and brute industrial effort. This formidable fellow walked out of the building with me, and said as we were parting, "Do you know calculus?"

I admitted that I didn't.

"You had better learn it," he said. "It's the language God talks."

Calculus

I never forgot Feynman's admonition, promising myself that I would get at calculus once I had written my big war novel, which I thought might take four or five years. It became two novels, each about a thousand pages long, and the task engulfed my life from my late forties well into my sixties, the better part of two decades. Toward the end I had a strong sense of racing the calendar to finish it before I died. All that while, the language God talks had to wait.

After that I did make several separate attempts to learn calculus, all recorded in a loose-leaf notebook which I still have. I tried self-teaching out of books with titles like *Calculus Made Easy*. I picked up and skimmed freshman texts in college bookstores, hoping to come across one that might help a mathematical ignoramus like me, who had spent his college years in the humanities—i.e., literature and philosophy—in an adolescent quest for the meaning of existence, little knowing that calculus, which I had heard of as a difficult bore leading nowhere, was the language God talks; or as one noted Jewish microbiologist, also a Torah scholar, commented to me with a grin, "His other language." I even engaged a tutor, an Israeli, figuring to improve my spoken Hebrew while learning calculus. A dumb idea, and I advanced in neither. Lastly, desperately, I got permission to audit a high-school course in calculus. I actually hung on with the teenagers for a couple of months, but I fell too far behind and had to withdraw, with a few farewell words to them about the preciousness of knowing calculus. As I was walking out of the classroom, a patter of applause surprised me; a sympathy hand, in showbiz parlance, for the defeated departing old codger.

In short, calculus remains a thick glass wall between me and most truths in Feynman's world where he hears God talk.

Gell-Mann

The Nobel laureate Murray Gell-Mann, Feynman's colleague and rival at Caltech, was no man to mince words, and he once observed that the gap between a person who understood quantum mechanics and one who did not was arguably wider than the difference between a human being and a great ape. On the other hand, Feynman is on the record as having said, "Nobody understands quantum mechanics." We have here what is called in Talmudic discourse, which I know pretty well, a sort of *Plugta d'tanoi,* that is, a standoff of the sages. Obviously I have to hope that the weight is with Feynman. As it happens, I know Murray Gell-Mann, and we have chatted some in a social vein. I did try once or twice to raise serious matters with him, but gave up. His responses, while not impolite, hinted that an orangutan was getting a bit too familiar.

Feynman was kinder. We met one summer years later at the Aspen Institute, a think tank high in the Colorado Rockies, and we took to lunching together and going on long walks. He did most of the talking: about his own work in physics, about quantum mechanics (making it seem momentarily almost understandable), and about philosophy, of which he was acidly scornful. His father, a dealer in uniforms, evidently a man with a restless inquiring mind, had greatly influenced him. Not much interested in novels or novel-writing, he perked up when I mentioned that I studied the Talmud daily. Feynman respected the Talmud as a "wonderful book," though he knew little about it. So I laid out for him an obscure abstruse problem that I had just struggled through. He listened keenly, thought for a moment, then rapped out the correct classic solution, and when I said he had hit it he was mighty pleased with himself. Would that Gell-Mann, with his imposing mind, had been inclined to loosen up like that. I treasure the memory of those illuminating lunches and walks.

My library contains whole shelves of science books for the common reader. I have read an amazing amount of the stuff. I may know nearly as much about modern science as one of Gell-Mann's anthropoids can grasp. Gell-Mann himself has written a long generous book in that vein, *The*

Quark and the Jaguar, which I have read cover to cover with much interest, and some labor. There is a book by Feynman, too, *Six Easy Pieces,* treating opaque topics like gravitation and quantum theory in his brisk native New York style. These pieces are excerpted from his renowned *Feynman Lectures on Physics,* a three-volume work impenetrable to untrained minds. I know, because I bought the oversize red paperbacks of the *Lectures,* and butted at those stone walls for weeks. *Six Easy Pieces* is deceptively accessible; in some swift turns of the talk one has to hang on for dear life.

Einstein too wrote such books, not very good ones. Explaining himself to the laity was not the forte of this man of the ages. Followers like James Jeans and Arthur Eddington voiced his epochal views in popular books, and scientists can even put out big bestsellers, like James Watson's *The Double Helix* and Stephen Hawking's *A Brief History of Time.* Hawking heeded his editor's warning, "Every equation you include cuts your readership in half," and his book contains only one, $E = mc^2$. Sure enough it sold like hotcakes. I bought a copy myself. The going gets pretty bumpy in Hawking even without equations, and when I slogged through to the end, I wondered how many other book buyers had honestly made it all the way. Still, I had gotten more than my money's worth in hard-won glimpses of the new cosmology.

Science writing is standard newspaper fare today.

Science magazines and websites abound, some sober, some jazzy, compacting the latest advances in cosmology and the biosciences into digestible English. It goes without saying that from the Nobel laureate like Gell-Mann who stoops to write a book for plain folk, to the columnist who scavenges *Nature* and *Science* to bang out his or her humble Sunday stint, they all know calculus. One and all, they have the advantage, in that respect, of the author of this little book which, adopting Feynman's metaphor, aspires to suggest that the stage may not be too big for the drama. Clearly I will not be talking down to the reader, not one bit, for by and large I address those like me on the wrong side of the mathematical glass wall.

What I write here is rooted in what I know of God's other language. Like many a Jewish Nobel laureate, Feynman speaks about religion from the wrong side of a very different glass wall, the Bible. There he has most of today's Jewry as company, including Murray Gell-Mann, for the Bible has long been waning as the core of a Jewish upbringing, a way of life once handed from father to son down the millennia, rooted in an epic history and an encyclopedic literature; a practical guide to the insoluble mysteries, brief joys, harsh blows, and everyday workings of a human existence. That upbringing survives here and there among our people, but most Jewish babies—in Israel, in America, in all the diaspora—are born today into the world view of Feynman and Gell-Mann; and a Nobel colleague of theirs, the physicist Steven Weinberg, has written lucid books in which the insoluble mysteries loom especially large, most of all the old agnostic paradox of an orderly universe without seeming purpose.

Order and Purpose

The world begins for a baby, so says William James, as "a big blooming buzzing confusion," a convincing surmise, though what is really going on in a baby's mind we know mainly by the screaming or the smiling. The baby has to sort out the confusion all by himself, little by little, experience by experience. He is bound to discern, very dimly at first, some kind of order and purpose in things, such as a nearby warm nipple when he feels hunger. This sense of order and purpose deepens and broadens as he picks up the basics of being alive. In time he starts to respond to baby talk. He obeys or balks at commands. The great day comes when he stands erect and takes a few faltering steps, his eyes agleam with wholly human pride which he can't yet express.

Once he does find his tongue, the sorting out process races ahead. He hounds both parents with one word, his prime sorter-out of order and purpose, "Why?" Sooner or later comes the leap to the big, the inexorable *Why,* which occurs to only one animal on earth: "Why am I here?", or in a more usual phrasing, "Where did I come from?" If you are an up-to-date liberated parent you are apt to leave God out of it, nor will you employ—it goes without saying— the antiquated dodges of stork or cabbage leaf. You will no doubt explain about sperm and ovum, and perhaps about penis and vagina, also about DNA, and maybe a little about natural selection. All that time your child will be looking you in the eye with a pure trusting gaze, and if you have a truthful bone in your body you will be embarrassed. With all the stunning modern discoveries in cosmology and the biosciences, you really don't know the answer. Nobody does. Not the unbeliever, not the believer. Faith is hope, not fact.

Yet every generation has to make a pass at an answer, and so does every father or mother. Feynman's rejection of religion as an answer to the child's question exhilarates me, and has in fact sparked this book, because I so largely agree with him. He is awed and exuberant, as I am, at the grandeur of the far-reaching universe, full of love, as I am, of our tiny enchanting Earth. He is my kind of agnostic, a votary of Democritus, the laughing philosopher who saw the world as a product only of "atoms and the void," which was quite enough to his Greek taste, because he found the world as it exists so pleasurable and beautiful. Like Democritus, Feynman finds the world as such "fantastically marvelous."

Weinberg

Now Weinberg, in his widely read book, *The First Three Minutes,* has put the bleaker agnostic picture with stark oft-quoted eloquence: "The more the universe seems comprehensible, the more it also seems pointless.... The effort to understand the universe is one of the very few things that lifts human life a little above the level of farce, and gives it some of the grace of tragedy."

No laughing philosopher, Weinberg. The human quest for Order and Purpose, which begins with the infant at the comforting nipple, ends for Weinberg in bafflement at the wondrous Order he sees in the universe, and despair at the comfortless absence of Purpose. The wondering child's ultimate sorter-out—WHY?—has haunted and hunted this eminent scientist to a dead end.

In *Facing Up,* a book of his essays, a photo of a granite statue serves as both jacket art and frontispiece.* Massive and stiff, the figure stares straight at the sky, head tilted far back, a defiant unshattered Ozymandias. This is Tycho Brahe, the sixteenth-century astronomer, memorialized in stone on the remote Danish island where he worked. The image resonates in Weinberg's spirit, for he calls himself a "devout secularist," and in his sardonic essay "A Designer Universe?"

---

* *Steven Weinberg,* Facing Up: Science and Its Cultural Adversaries *(Cambridge, MA: Harvard University Press, 2003).*

he sets out to inflict mayhem on the Argument from Design, theology's old fall-back proof of God's existence. He himself has not only discerned the Order in the cosmos, he won his Nobel Prize by more exactly defining it. He knows whereof he speaks, and here is how he concludes the essay: "One of the great achievements of science has been, if not to make it impossible for intelligent people to be religious, then at least to make it possible for them not to be religious. We should not retreat from this accomplishment."

I would shake hands on that accomplishment with Steven Weinberg.

My Lame Paws

As a Columbia undergraduate, imbibing the Greek philosophy, comparative religion, and general humanism of the noted core curriculum, I rode the subway to the Bronx once a week to study the Talmud with my grandfather. The Talmud is a hard grind in Aramaic, and to lighten up things I would now and then venture an agnostic prod at some tender point of our faith—say, Joshua's stopping the sun and the moon. Grandpa would respond with good-natured scorn, stroking his full gray beard, "Where are you creeping with your lame paws?" It was more pungent in Yiddish, but you get the idea. That question has been occurring to me as I write these words. Disqualified as I have described myself for getting into these deep murky waters—no academic credentials to speak of, no mathematics beyond half-forgotten algebra—where am I creeping with this venturesome causerie?

Fair question, reader, so let me invite you into the workshop of an old author still creating stories, my work, my intermittent despair, and my lifelong fun. With a new novel recently published and another on the stocks, I have stepped back from my desk, drawn breath, and glanced around the shop for overlooked items. One folder labeled *A Child's Garden of God* lies to a side, more scuffed than most, in which for years I've been stashing false starts on the answer offered by the Bible (insofar as I can grasp it) to the grand *Why* of the child and of stumped agnostics. No wonder I have kept putting it off! A big bite.

Newton summed up his lifework in well-known words:

> I know not what I seem to the world, but to myself I seem to have been only like a boy playing on the seashore, and diverting myself in now and then finding a smoother pebble or a prettier shell, whilst the great ocean of truth lay all undiscovered before me.

It was this child having fun on the beach who came upon the smoother pebble called the calculus (oddly, the word means "pebble"), enabling thinkers after him to venture far out on that ocean of truth, toward a distant shore of final theory which, as they keep learning to their gloomy puzzlement, ever recedes. Isaac Newton not only found Feynman's "language God talks," he also mastered God's other language, and studied and wrote on the Hebrew Bible, a fact that embarrasses some scientists. Newton put Feynman's dictum on calculus, which he called "fluxions," in plain words suited to his own faith, *"God created everything by number, weight, and measure."* An agnostic paraphrase for our day might be, *"All that is truly knowable is knowable only by number, weight, and measure."* Or as James Jeans put it, *"God is a mathematician."*

God as Irony

A byname for God in Aramaic is *Atik Yomin,* Ancient of Days. Einstein now and then spoke of his work as wresting secrets from *Der Alter,* the Old One. He was being puckish, of course, and so no doubt was Feynman in calling calculus "the language God talks." Neither savant meant the God of the Bible, the God of Abraham, Isaac, and Jacob, my grandfather's God, and his father's, and my father's, and mine, and Pascal's, and Faraday's, and Newton's. The God of modern scientists by and large is a figure of speech, an ironic flourish. Darwin himself sometimes wrote of God in a religious mode, but in the present day such literal usage tends to fade out. Feynman, Gell-Mann, Weinberg, and their peers accept Newton's incomparable stature and shrug off his piety, on the kindly thought that the old man got into the game too early. He did not even know for sure that light travels, for in his *Opticks* he refers to the travel of light as an interesting conjecture, based on the equations of a Danish astronomer for the orbit of Jupiter. To the real numbing size of the universe, the naive time-bound giant was blind.

Feynman in three lectures on science and religion dances lightfoot around this grand theme, and ends by endorsing the ethics of a papal encyclical while waving off its pious core. As for Gell-Mann, he seems to see nothing to discuss in this entire God business, and in the index to *The Quark and the Jaguar* God goes unmentioned. Life he calls a "complex adaptive system" which produces interesting phenomena such as the jaguar and Murray Gell-Mann, who discovered the quark. Gell-Mann is a Nobel-class tackler of problems, but for him the existence of God is not one of them.

Weinberg is different, a quarreler with God in the vein of Job, who confronts the Lord straight on with that everlasting religious challenge, the existence of senseless evil in the world of an omnipotent Creator. Weinberg goes further and tells Newton's Creator to his face that on the available evidence, he is a figment. Stendhal put the agnostic view so, "The only excuse for God is that he does not exist," but Weinberg is too serious a thinker to let the Creator off with a Gallic witticism. He is angry at the horrible record

17

of fanatic deeds done in God's name down the generations, and he will not tolerate facile philosophizing of God back into existence. Better tell it like it is! Newton's God is not there, so no supernatural being can be blamed for the evils of the meaningless human condition, which rises to tragedy only in mankind's dogged gropings for final truth, as in the Book of Job and in Weinberg's writings.

The Stage and the Drama

In dealing with ultimate mystery, one is thrown back on irony and metaphor: the stage and the drama, the quark and the jaguar, the boy and the pebble, the child and the garden. Here is one more metaphor that emboldens me, ill-equipped as I am, to take on at last the big bite. Picture a man who has lived most of his working life in exile, say an American mining engineer in Western Australia. He marries a Perth lady, and forty years slip swiftly and pleasurably by. Comes time for retirement. On balance he decides to live out his years in his native Nevada, and knowing that he may never look on Australia again, he takes one last tour around this remote island continent he has come to love. For the rest of his days he will cherish his memories of that bittersweet farewell.

This lovely sunlit Earth is an exile all of us must leave, one after the other, to return whence we came. I embark here on a tour of our beautiful little Australia in space, this child's garden of God, at a pause in my storytelling, anticipating a sure farewell at an uncertain time. I invite the reader to join me. On the wing as I am, it behooves me to write out these thoughts while I can, and I won't pretend I write to please only myself. All my working life I have written for readers, and I do so now, be they many or few.

Is the stage really too big for the drama, as Feynman asserted? I believe it's possible to disagree, and that is the main theme of this book. At the outset, let us take a fresh look at the stage, and start with a grand moment in the drama.

CHAPTER TWO

Outward Bound

The Great Day

When mankind first left the earth I was there. A friendly *National Geographic* executive invited me to witness the liftoff of Apollo 11 from Cape Canaveral on July 16, 1969, a day when the Cape buzzed with the powerful and the famous.

How different it was to watch an Apollo launch at the Cape, rather than on TV! No warm-voiced avuncular Walter Cronkite on the small screen, no space-suited astronauts going off to their fate with waves and smiles, no close-ups of the towering snowy Saturn V shaft wisping vapor, no clueless interviewers killing time by badgering scientists and engineers. None of that, just a long wait under a baking Florida sun on a wooden bench in a crowded stand; the rocket gleaming white and diminutive at a safe distance,

Mission Control droning from a loudspeaker overhead: "Five...four...three...two...one....We have ignition."

Flames shoot out from under the rocket! White smoke billows, and the faraway colossus rises without a sound on a growing pillar of fire. Tears start to my eyes. A roar comes rolling at us and over us, a roar beyond any I have ever heard, a primal roar out of Genesis, Adam tearing loose from the Garden's grip, and after the sound the shaking and shuddering of the earth....

The Saturn accelerates, dwindling away up into the blue....

And that was it!

Apollo 11 riveted the world because, for one thing, nobody could then predict what the surface of the moon would be like. Nobody! Sober scientists worried that the first astronaut to venture outside the lander might sink and get swallowed up by the fine space dust accumulated over aeons, and perish as in a quicksand. Four days later, in shadowy live TV pictures, came the reassuring answer—a helmeted man backing down out of the spidery module on a short ladder, planting a Robinson Crusoe footprint on the moon, and sinking in not at all as he declared, "That's one small step for a man, one giant leap for mankind."

Neil Armstrong might have uttered instead words less noble but no less apt, when his boot touched the moon:

"We win!" For the Apollo program was created to beat the Soviet Union to the moon, nothing else.

Apollo by a Nose

That was the sporting side of the Cold War, the lunatic face-off of the two superpowers during forty frightening years I lived through, rattling rockets with hydrogen-bomb warheads at each other, thirty hair-trigger minutes away from a flameout of civilization. Neither government ever declared the moon race a *race*. Not at all! Rocket engineering now made it possible to get men to the moon and back, and since—as George Mallory said of Everest—the moon was *there*, we were going there. So both sides feigned, but of course it was just a race, a race for mortal stakes of global preeminence, and the whole world knew that.

The Russians had seized a walloping head start in October 1957 by launching Sputnik, the first man-made space satellite, a metal sphere no bigger than a basketball which went sailing and beeping round and round the globe. Today, when the Soviet Union has long been defunct, when satellites in numbers are up there serving as flying switchboards and surveillance cameras, the magnitude of that surprise half a century ago is hardly imaginable. Yet I well remember what a shocking setback Sputnik was to America's national prestige and sense of security; no Pearl

Harbor or 9/11 to be sure, yet a bone-shaking blow. The U.S. military had been pottering with rocketry for years, playing out clumsy failures on TV, and all that time the Russians had been secretly cooking up Sputnik.

President Eisenhower went on the air to pooh-pooh Sputnik as a trivial little stunt, whereupon the Russians forthwith lofted a half-ton satellite with a live dog in it! The giddy American media dubbed this one Muttnik, making sheepish fun of the communist space triumph, while European experts snidely opined that the United States could never catch up to the Soviet Union. The President's assumed calm soothed nobody. Congress appropriated a frenzied billion dollars* to improve the country's scientific education (not specifying how), and still more funds for a new agency, the National Aeronautics and Space Administration—our old friend NASA, that is—to get America the hell up to the moon first.

But a stern chase is a long chase, Navy byword. The humiliation of the United States went on for years. American space efforts publicly fizzled, the frequent Soviet fizzles (as we now know) went unannounced and undetected, and when John Kennedy succeeded Eisenhower the country was still nowhere in the undeclared race. In the spring of 1961 a Russian cosmonaut, Yuri Gagarin, rocketed into orbit clear around the earth in 108 minutes,

---

* *Then a lot of money. —HW, 2009*

the first human being in space, an instant world hero. A few days later America's first astronaut, Alan Shepard, also shot up into space, and his tiny Mercury capsule plopped down in the Atlantic on schedule, fifteen minutes after it went up.

That probably did it. John Kennedy summoned a special joint session of Congress, to deliver a grave nine-point address on the state of the nation and of the whole world. I heard that speech. Only in point nine did the young president touch on space. Then, with all his casual charm and in that beguiling Boston accent, he remarked, "I believe we should go to the moon," and he proposed funding a gigantic crash program to send a man there and bring him back within ten years, by mobilizing American science and industry on the scale of the Manhattan Project, this time in full world view. Congress readily complied. The Apollo program sprang into existence. Eight years later, an American stepped out on the moon. No Russian yet has. In short, we won.

But there was more to the success than that. In Apollo 11 a showy actor, half hero and half clown, the primate science calls *Homo sapiens,* made a spectacular debut on Richard Feynman's Big Stage with a leap between two celestial bodies and a great opening line: an instance of what Americans can do when aroused.

Der Fuehrer's Folly

Yet it is pretty well forgotten that both moon programs were in fact spearheaded neither by an American nor a Russian, but by two Germans.

Back in 1945, the Red Army rolling toward Berlin scooped up Hitler's V-2 rocket scientists, engineers, and technicians, some five thousand in all. A project chief, Wernher von Braun, contrived to slip off with some of his key staff to the American side, but his obscure co-chief, one Helmut Groettrup, was less agile. In virtual Soviet captivity, Groettrup designed engines that powered Sputnik, Muttnik, and in part the moon rockets, while Stalin was retrieving Russian scientists from the gulags where they were rotting away. Once they took over they made a brilliant, heartbreaking effort that might well have won, but blockhead Marxist bureaucrats hampered them and frittered away the long Soviet lead, while Wernher von Braun, riding a surge of all-out American technology in a blaze of publicity, booted home the victor. Incidentally, since von Braun was so useful to our side, the many deaths of slave laborers in his underground rocket factories were soft-pedalled; as when Hitler attacked Russia and forced the Red Army to fight on the Allied side, Franklin Roosevelt soft-pedalled Stalin's mass slaughters, and flooded lend-lease munitions to him. Way of the world.

Big science demands political muscle as well as huge expenditures, and Adolf Hitler had lavished both on his V-2 rockets, a momentously stupid decision. Nazi Germany had started the war with a wide lead not only in rocketry but in nuclear physics. German physicists had achieved fission in 1938 well before anyone else, and even under the Nazis, German science and industry remained formidable. What motivated the Manhattan Project was exactly the fear that the Germans were well along in building an atomic bomb for Hitler. Had he in fact backed the right terror weapon, who can say how history might have gone? Providentially for mankind, Der Fuehrer was not only—in Churchill's picturesque rhetoric—a bloodthirsty maniac, he was a pigheaded maniac. He never saw anything in the German uranium effort, which after the war was discovered to be pathetically puny, and he bet the farm on his darling V-2s, which eventually set random fires in London and killed a lot of civilians. It is a haunting enigma of twentieth-century history that an advanced Western nation adored this grisly madman and obeyed his orders to his last hour, when he shot himself in a Berlin bunker under Red Army artillery bombardment. The victors seized on the dead monster's rocket weapon and improved it to run the big race, won by the American team I watched soaring off into space from Florida.

There were six more Apollo missions. Only Apollo 13 attracted any comparable attention, when part of the spacecraft blew up fifty thousand miles from the moon. For a while the astronauts seemed doomed, and that made for a television cliff-hanger; but the crew were rocket engineers as well as space explorers, so they got themselves home, and the happy ending inspired a hit movie. After Apollo 17, with more astronaut teams trained and raring to fly and more Saturn Vs ready to go, the mighty project abruptly shut down, out of money and—as the media slang has it—legs.

So the curtain dropped on Act One of the cosmic drama about the creatures that struggle for good and evil: *Homo sapiens, Outward Bound.*

Entr'acte: Armstrong

Sometime after Apollo 11 I happened to catch Neil Armstrong on TV, doing a Chrysler commercial in civvies. Well!! *Homo sapiens,* peak of evolution, American icon, star of the cosmic drama, in the toils of Madison Avenue! I decided that Armstrong did not have to do this, he should write a book instead, a sure blockbuster, and I would help him any way I could. Novelists have their nutty side, so next day I actually phoned my *National Geographic* friend, who knew Armstrong well, and asked for a meeting of the three of us.

Encountered on Earth over lunch at the *Geographic,*

Armstrong was pleasant, reserved, willing to listen. A Navy man, he may have read *The Caine Mutiny* and wondered what the author wanted of him. In the flesh this handsome rather pale man was still an astral presence, at least to me. Those remote keen eyes, I felt, had looked upon the face of the Lord. But there I was, so I made my lame pitch: a book by the first American to set foot on the moon should be read by youth yet unborn, it would be a great inspiration, etc., etc., etc. Armstrong heard me out and shrugged off the notion. Apollo was a team endeavor first to last, he said, the engineering achievements were the main thing, and they were on record. As for the rest, the story of the astronauts was well-known, and his personal experiences did not matter. End of my effort to tell a figure of history how to run his life.

In retrospect I can't really regret my brash folly, for I did get to lunch with the actor who played *Homo sapiens* in his cosmic debut. Offstage, as it were, Armstrong was a calm professional with no public relations flair and a striking absence of superstar ego. Masked behind that quiet persona, all the same, were the resolve, tenacity, and moral force of the ace among American aces elected to step first on the moon. Masked too were the level head and lightning judgment of a pilot who, a quarter million miles from Earth, with ninety seconds of fuel left, bypassed the designated landing site and glided over the moon looking for a better place to touch down.

Act Two?

So, outer space breached! The conquest of a new frontier
brilliantly begun! Moon voyage dream of stargazers, poets,
storytellers down the ages come true! Cold chaste goddess
of the night ravished by an outward-bound primate, and
fled for all time weeping to the dark side of the moon!
Whither now, *Homo sapiens?* What does NASA do for an
encore in space pioneering?

Answer, plenty! A huge new agency now existed with
a fat budget to match. Not since Galileo and the Medicis
had such a window of political heft and hard cash opened
on new science. Heady days for astronomers, astrophysicists, and space engineers! Next stop for our space fron-
tiersmen? Mars, of course, well within reach of Apollo's
rocket technology. Problems, to be sure: How would the
astronauts—for all their right stuff, human like the rest
of us—endure two years or more of cosmic radiation in
zero gravity? Would their bones soften, could their DNA
unravel? Needed thought. Prudent first step: Build a space
station to orbit the earth, and a cheap reusable spacecraft
to shuttle astronauts there and back. Observe the effects of
prolonged weightlessness and cosmic radiation on them as
they do experiments in space science, floating for months
in near-zero gravity. Then and only then, on to Mars.

As for unmanned projects, exciting ideas abounded on

the drawing boards; robot probes of all the planets, with cameras to send back blockbuster photographs for the world to marvel at, and advanced instruments to learn up close what was really there. The crown jewel of the unmanned program, the "Large Space Telescope," would orbit outside the blurry air we breathe, to give us our first clear look at the stars mankind would one day be exploring. When Apollo 11 planted a simulated Stars and Stripes on the moon, together with a plaque signed by the astronauts and President Nixon—*Here men from the planet Earth first set foot upon the moon July 1969, A. D. We came in peace for all mankind*—these projects were well along, and NASA was riding high.

No sooner had the last moonwalkers landed back home, than President Nixon axed the Large Space Telescope: too expensive. The organized anguished howl of astronomers and astrophysicists could be shrugged off, but a letter-writing blizzard from a sizeable public devoted to television's *Star Trek* was serious business. The telescope was okayed, otherwise NASA had bumped to earth with its moonwalkers. Race won, crash budget finished, start of the agency's annual sweat for appropriations. Down the years since, the robot probes of the solar system have been paying their way by wowing the world—and more importantly, Congress—with gorgeous close-ups of giant Jupiter, its Red Spot and its moons, Saturn and its ever-fascinating rings, and so on, while delivering significant new planetary science. Moreover, NASA's visionary Origins program—*Where have we come from? Are we alone?*—has found earthlike planets circling the distant stars, and another program has landed two six-wheeled crawlers on Mars that have explored and televised red rocky panoramas much like our Death Valley and Grand Canyon, reporting traces of water and even elusive hints of conditions possibly suitable for life.

Yet manned spaceflight, the primary mission for which Congress created NASA, has languished. In 2005 a seasoned space engineer, Michael Griffin, startled his first press conference as NASA's new administrator by announcing, "NASA lost its way in the 1970s, and took the wrong path. We have to get back to the right way." To the agency chiefs he spoke gruff words: "The American public will support only a NASA that goes somewhere and does something"; free translation, "We head for Mars pronto, troops, or we're dead." Griffin had coauthored a study by eight space scientists, "Extending Human Presence into the Solar System," and President Bush (the younger) had used its findings to issue a new Space Exploration Initiative, at which NASA's scientists quaked, for the study phased out shuttle and space station to go for Mars via the moon, *while staying within the agency's current budget.* To fund the costly two-phase leap to Mars, other programs would have to be curtailed, stretched out, postponed, or dropped. In effect, the drama

Homo sapiens, Outward Bound was closing out of town for drastic revision of Act Two.

Griffin's "Wrong Path": A Reminiscence

What was this wrong path? In short, the very first step: a space station and a cheap reusable spacecraft.

Way back in April 1981, as I well remember, an enormous TV audience of taxpayers like me awaited the launch of the first new American spacecraft since Apollo. On the Cape Canaveral launchpad, a bizarre monster wisped prelaunch vapor, about half as tall as Apollo's Saturn V rocket, clearly both a rocket and an airplane, the SHUTTLE; a thing sui generis, "the most complex machine ever built," so the agency publicists proudly put it. Called *Columbia,* it flamed and roared off into a two-day test flight; and the TV audience was almost as big when it returned, for it had to plunge at orbit speed from outer space into the incendiary friction of Earth's atmosphere. What protection did the strange hybrid have, its rocket elements discarded, only the plane doing the reentry? Walter Cronkite assured us that heat-resistant tiles lining its nose and wings would suffice, but when the pilot's chatter from *Columbia* abruptly ceased, Cronkite too stopped talking, no doubt holding his breath like the rest of us. As *Columbia*'s chatter resumed and our hearts beat again, an aircraft of a peculiar configuration came in sight; and to the televised rejoicing of everyone in Mission Control, and the cheers of the emergency crews waiting with firefighting gear, it glided to earth and released a drogue parachute for a flawless landing.

Two more shuttles, *Discovery* and *Challenger,* came on line. The missions, each about two weeks long, got to be routine. The launches and reentries dropped out of the news. Live TV pictures of shirtsleeved astronauts floating in the roomy shuttle, eating or experimenting or talking to Earth, were brief novelties, and their pioneering spacewalks, suited up and tethered to the spacecraft, at first got wide coverage. However, their invariable success soon made for yawns, though each mission was exactly as perilous as the first one. NASA's manned spaceflight program had been out of whack from the start, when President Nixon approved only *half* the project: a shuttle, yes; a space station, no, not yet. Even for the "cheap reusable spacecraft," the appropriation was so meager that it had to be eked out with Air Force funding. The Air Force was mighty interested, of course, in the military aspects of space, but wanted value for its money.

The upshot was a custom-built space machine with a dual mission. Air Force purposes tended to be classified or blacked out in top secrecy. NASA's science goals required media visibility and public support. The shuttle metamorphosed into an engineering marvel at a far stretch of human ingenuity and American technology; perhaps indeed the most complex machine ever built, its design a web of innovation and compromise. Unlike other aircraft, for instance, the shuttle could not use reverse thrust of engines on landing; super-powerful brakes had to bring it to a stop, hence a drogue parachute to assist.

In 1984 President Reagan drew renewed attention to the program by announcing a Teacher in Space Project. NASA would train a schoolteacher as an astronaut, to stimulate interest of the young in space by giving lessons from an orbiting shuttle. Eleven thousand teachers volunteered. Christa McAuliffe, an attractive mother of two from New Hampshire, was chosen, and her first mission provided fresh grist about the space mission for television and press. On the day of the launch I was in the synagogue at morning minyan, when a latecomer reported a rumor that the shuttle had exploded! I raced home in disbelief, turned on the TV, and with a sick heart watched the catastrophe played out over and over: *Challenger* rising in a perfect liftoff on a column of fire, soaring away into a clear blue sky, then a ball of yellow flame bursting in air, and a crooked trail of white smoke following the spacecraft debris down to the sea.

The country was in shock. Reagan appointed a Presidential Commission to probe the disaster. Former Secretary of State William Rogers was chairman, Neil Armstrong was his deputy, and among its members was Richard Feynman.

Feynman's Cold Water*

A theoretical physicist, a chalk-and-blackboard man, Feynman knew nothing of space engineering. He reluctantly responded to the call, cancelled his commitments for months ahead, and spent a long day at Caltech's Jet Propulsion Laboratory, sponging up shuttle technology from the engineers. Next day in Washington, at an informal get-together of the commission's members in Rogers' office, he took a shine to one General Kutyna, resplendent in Air Force uniform. The uniform didn't impress Feynman—after all, his father had dealt in uniforms—but when the meeting ended, he heard the general ask someone where the nearest Metro station was, and that impressed him. A big-shot general who had no car and driver at his beck and call was his kind of guy. Next day at the board's first encounter with NASA leaders, under bright TV lights, Feynman was sitting next to the general. Before the meeting began Kutyna muttered, "Copilot to pilot. Comb your hair." Feynman responded, "Pilot to copilot, can I borrow your comb?" The two men somehow hit it off from the start.

Otherwise this first meeting had depressed and discouraged Feynman. He had gained a good technical grasp of

---

* *Feynman's detailed account is in* What Do You Care What Other People Think? *(New York: Norton, 1988).*

the *Challenger* problem at the Jet Propulsion Lab, and was eager to attack it in depth; but he had heard only bland generalities, and the news that next week the commission would go to Cape Canaveral for a briefing, i.e., a mere dog and pony show. Rogers vetoed Feynman's impulse to fly instead to the Johnson Space Center in Houston to talk to the engineers—"not an orderly procedure"—so Feynman asked at least to visit NASA's engineers right there in Washington. At another veto, the bumptious Nobel laureate raised a row, the chairman gave in, and next day Feynman crossed the street from his hotel to NASA headquarters, where the engineers were friendly and free with disclosures.

The essential misjudgment of the launch, he soon discerned, might have been ghastly in its simplicity. A cold snap had dropped the mercury at Cape Canaveral to the 20s that fatal January morning, and the shuttle was not supposed to go up in weather colder than 53 degrees. Bad enough, but what was the exact flaw or failure that might have caused the explosion? They told him that the hybrid had five rocket components, all suspect: the three gigantic main engines, and two solid-fuel booster rockets. The engines were fueled from a towering tank that was discarded en route to orbit. The booster rockets quickly burned out at launch and parachuted into the sea, to be recovered and disassembled for repair; and their joints on reassembly were sealed with so-called O-rings of rubber.

Feynman was scrawling notes on all this in his hotel room when General Kutyna telephoned. William Rogers had asked him to tell Dr. Feynman *not* to go to NASA, after all. Feynman shrugged that off, inwardly amused. Kutyna went on, "Say, I was working on the O-rings in my carburetor this morning, and I got to thinking about the shuttle. It took off when the weather was 28, 29 degrees. You're a professor. What, sir, would be the effect of cold on O-rings?"

"Oh, well, make them stiff, of course."

Kutyna said no more. He didn't have to. The theoretical physicist caught the hint. A skilled practical joker—at Los Alamos he had beguiled tedium by picking security locks and cracking safes—Feynman resolved to try an end run around Washington's stifling procedures. He obtained at NASA a small strip of O-ring rubber from a model of the shuttle, and tested it in a glass of ice water. Sure enough, at 32 degrees it stiffened like wood. At the next public meeting of the commission, where for the first time NASA's launch personnel were testifying about the disaster before a packed press corps and a massed battery of TV cameras, he saw to it that a glass of ice water was on the table beside his microphone. Into this glass he dropped the rubber strip.

When a launch manager started briefing the board, Feynman reached for his microphone button to quiz him. General Kutyna leaned over, muttered, "Pilot to copilot, not just yet," and pointed out the O-rings page in their briefing book. As soon as the manager reached that page, Feynman shot questions at him about the temperature on the launch morning; and lifting the wet rubber from the ice water, he demonstrated how inflexible it was at 32 degrees. "I believe this has some significance for our problem," Feynman remarked. Secretary Rogers struck in at once, "That is something we will certainly consider at length in our session on the weather," and told the flummoxed manager to proceed to the next topic. Of course the media caught on. Feynman's coup de theatre was the big story on the evening news and in the next day's headlines; and the chalk-and-blackboard man became better known to the public overnight, than a lifetime of brilliant physics plus the Nobel Prize had made him.

Three months later, all the board signed off on a summary report with a set of unanimous conclusions and recommendations—all, that is, except Richard Feynman. The board member assigned by Rogers to collate their varied views, a physicist who worked in Washington, had used not a single word of Feynman's observations! Pressed to explain, he could only come up with shifty evasions that convinced Feynman his strong views were being shunted aside. He threatened to remove his name from the report, and a compromise was reached; his comments, heavily edited, would be attached as an appendix. His memoir ends with this appendix and a postscript called "Afterthoughts" in which he levels about his ice-water feat. An astronaut friend had told General Kutyna, he discloses, that the lack of resilience in the O-rings at low temperatures was known at NASA but wasn't being talked about. Kutyna wanted to bring to light this clue to the disaster, but without jeopardizing the astronaut. "His solution," Feynman wryly writes, "was to get the professor excited about it, and his plan worked perfectly."

Rattled off like the whole memoir in his brash style, the appendix is a penetrating analysis of NASA's problems at the interface of science and politics, a sort of defining document of Act Two. At no time does Feynman disparage the eternal human urge to explore, nor the American pioneering spirit at the heart of NASA's mandate. On the contrary, he tells of being moved near tears by a film of the agency's wondrous accomplishments in space science and technology. When he went to Washington he had long been fighting cancer. A year later he was dead. Summoned in his waning days to do a patriotic service, Richard Feynman suspended his last work in physics, poked around to find out what had happened to *Challenger,* and told the truth in a drench of cold water.

Columbia *Disintegrates*

The Manhattan Project was spawned to beat the Germans to the atomic bomb, and NASA was spawned to beat the

Soviets to the moon. These two juggernauts of American resolve commandeered vast holdings of land, erected enormous structures, raised battalions of high-powered personnel, and after they won their races, kept rolling down the years until they collided head-on in the Appropriations Bill of 1993 under President Clinton. Two big-ticket science items were bitterly debated in Congress: the atomic physicists' Superconducting Super Collider and NASA's Space Station. Many years earlier President Reagan in his laid-back way had given the green light to both, but this was Clinton's first year. He had made a campaign pledge to tighten the national budget, and one of the science behemoths had to go down. The super collider got the axe. America's lead in high-energy physics was lost to Europe.* The space station squeaked through by one vote; clearly, seven years after *Challenger*'s fall, Congress remained chilly about man in space; and funding continued so lean that when actual construction of the space station began in 1998, Japan, Canada, and Russia were chipping in as partners.

Meantime, the shuttle was redeeming itself with successful mission after mission; outstandingly, it lifted into orbit the Large Space Telescope, christened the *Hubble Telescope* to honor Edwin Hubble, hero of our next chapter, who first accurately measured Feynman's Big Stage. When the images from the half-billion-dollar instrument proved

---

* *My novel* A Hole in Texas *(New York: Little, Brown, 2004) is a rueful comedy on this grave theme.*

fuzzy because the mirror was out of focus, a media circus ensued; but once the shuttle astronauts did a long complex repair job, the images sprang forth sharp and brilliant, and the Hubble astounded the world with its powerful new reach far, far back into the depths of the early universe. NASA caught its breath, as it were, for a while, and the International Space Station was coming along well, when *Columbia,* the first of the shuttles and for two decades a steady workhorse, got into trouble.

Columbia's launch in January 2003 went awry. Debris broke off the insulation of the discardable fuel tank; nothing very new, but this was a pretty big chunk, and it hit a wing of the shuttle. A friend of mine was in the crew— Ilan Ram-on, the first Israeli astronaut—so I was following with concern the broadcast snatches of very calm talk between the crew and Mission Control, as the fifteen-day mission was carried out as planned. On reentry the damaged heat tiles failed, and through a hole in the wing's leading edge, atmosphere superheated by reentry speed entered the wing like a blowtorch, melting everything in its path. *Columbia* disintegrated, and in the loss of seven more lives the wrong path dead-ended. Two shuttles out of five had fallen. The three surviving machines were grounded for total overhaul—not retired, since America was committed by then to sixteen other countries to complete a "core" of the station, and only the shuttle had the cargo space and the thrust to lift the heavy stuff. Construction halted, and the small Russian Soyuz "lifeboat" serviced caretaker astronauts on the inert platform for three long years.

It was shortly before the overhauled *Discovery* went up on a test mission that Michael Griffin became administrator; and once again, large chunks of insulation broke off the fuel tank and struck the shuttle! *Discovery* survived to deliver its freight to the space station and got back to Earth safe, so NASA public relations announced a successful test. Griffin, a no-nonsense guy, grounded all three shuttles for another year. When *Discovery* went up once more, I saw him on TV, unshaven and resolute, telling a press conference that if the crew were endangered this time he'd abort the entire shuttle program. The spacecraft performed without incident, and the program was on again. Today (March 2009) the International Space Station is not only flourishing but expanding. A recent shuttle load included living quarters for two more astronauts, six in all. Griffin's goal to complete the "American core" by 2010 appears on track, after which NASA's remarkable if flawed hybrid spacecraft will pass into history.

L'Envoi: "Saturn by 1970!"

In the forty years since his dazzling Apollo debut, *Homo sapiens,* cosmic explorer, has gone nowhere, just circled Earth a few miles overhead, round and round and round.

The study that Michael Griffin coauthored—and that President George W. Bush leaned on to keep NASA alive—opens with a sober discussion of funding requirements, and concludes with two linked hardheaded facts about the human reach beyond the moon:

1. MARS IS THE END OF THE LINE. The numbers are all but unanswerable. A manned round-trip mission to Mars has to take about three years. Jupiter, the next planet outward, is roughly *ten times* as far, so a mission to a Jupiter moon would involve some *thirty years,* more than an astronaut's working lifetime. Saturn is twenty times as far as Mars, and so on outward.

2. TRAVEL BEYOND MARS WILL REQUIRE NUCLEAR-PROPELLED SPACECRAFT, NOT FEASIBLE IN THE FORESEEABLE FUTURE. This seductive possibility—the million-to-one ratio of nuclear to chemical energy—has long been known to physicists. The chemical energy in five gallons of gasoline, say, will take an automobile a hundred miles or so along a freeway; the nuclear energy in those same five gallons would thrust a spacecraft *a hundred million miles, or all the way to Mars.* The Griffin study sums up, concerning this tantalizing fact of nature, that it may prove useful only at a far distant time, when international comity allows for cooperation not now thinkable.

Yet in 1958, the first year of the post-Sputnik frenzy, a proposal to build a nuclear-powered spaceship actually got some federal funding. Project Orion it was called, brainchild of the atomic guru Stanislaus Ulam, who coinvented the hydrogen bomb. Ulam testified before Congress that his big spaceship would cruise with ease around the solar system propelled by atomic minibombs, detonating at intervals near a "pusher plate," which would absorb and soften the stupendous explosions so as not to jelly the astronauts. A model of Orion did fly—on chemical energy—and can be seen today at Washington's National Air and Space Museum. Several eminent physicists threw themselves into Orion heart and soul, their slogan, *"Saturn by 1970!"** If the idea sounds loony to the reader, remember that after Sputnik the panic was on, and no notion seemed too wild to consider; also that in the airless black void between the planets there would be no noise, no flame, no fallout, just a very hard *push* every now and then to zip Orion along.**

Far out? Of course. When Hitler was rampaging toward Moscow, and World War II looked lost because the United States was staying out of it, Winston Churchill reassured his cabinet, "America is a boiler!" Within the month Pearl Harbor lit off that boiler. Sixteen years later Sputnik lit it off again. Since then the boiler seems to have gone stone cold. Still, when all is said and done, Americans have walked on the moon, while other nations have given up trying or are in

---

* *Freeman Dyson,* Disturbing the Universe *(New York: Harper & Row, 1979).*

** *George Dyson,* Project Orion: The True Story of the Atomic Spaceship *(New York: Henry Holt and Company, 2002).*

the first dogged stages of attempting it. The Hubble Telescope, rescued by an American public devoted to dreams of exploring the stars, has revolutionized astrophysics and shaken up philosophy and religion. Apollo and the Hubble were the achievements of a bumbling, stumbling, brave Washington bureaucracy, the National Aeronautics and Space Administration.

Churchill said one thing more: "You can count on the Americans to do the right thing, after they have tried everything else."

Note: Freeman Dyson faulted this chapter, in vetting the manuscript, as mistaken on man in space and meager on the Russian space program. Dyson sees in beamed energy propulsion, powerful microwaves driving lightweight vehicles along "laser highways," a sober future for travel to Mars and beyond. The concept is in fact under international study and experiment today. As to the Russians, in truth they were years ahead of NASA with a space station, *Mir,* and a really "cheap, reusable spacecraft," *Soyuz.* Their cosmonauts throve on *Mir* and still hold the record for continuous months lived in space; and only *Soyuz* will be keeping the International Space Station alive for years while NASA phases out the shuttle and tools up for the moon and Mars. Other authorities disagree with Dyson on man in space; for instance, in Steven Weinberg's long scathing study "The Wrong Stuff," he puts down manned space programs as a profligate waste of scarce science funding (*New York Review of Books,* April 8, 2004). My chapter is a distillation of all I could learn in the writing, as it bore on my main theme.

CHAPTER THREE

How Big the Stage?

The Stagehands

Now there is in fact an energy other than nuclear, with which our star-trekking primate has already traveled far beyond Mars. It is the electric charge racing through the billion-threaded nerves of his brain.

A chimpanzee will pull a banana into his cage with a stick, and if the stick isn't long enough, he can fit two sticks together to get it.* This interesting fact bears on Feynman's Big Stage, for *Homo sapiens* in much the same way—so the animal behaviorists might well insist—has fitted pieces of glass into a tube, pointed the tube at the sky, and with it pulled in the measure of the universe.** Certainly the

---

* *Wolfgang Kohler,* The Mentality of the Apes *(New York: Routledge, 1978).*

** *Jared Diamond,* The Third Chimpanzee *(New York: HarperCollins, 1992).*

naked-eye cosmos of the ancients—and of our uncorrected common sense—dissolved once Galileo pricked it with his tube improved from a Dutch invention; and once Newton devised his "catadioptrical" mirror, as his amazed peers termed it, giving undistorted clarity to the view through the tube, no theoretical boundary remained to the brain's reach into space.

These tools of Galileo and Newton—the senior stage-hands, let's call them—were the merest by-products of their great work. The junior stagehands, George Ellery Hale and Henrietta Leavitt, gave their whole lives to the tube. In 1642, the year Galileo died, Newton was born, and Hale and Leavitt were both born in 1868; so two centuries separated the immortal seniors and the more or less unsung juniors. The history of astronomy is studded with resounding names, but by building principally on the work of these four—such is my perception, anyway—Edwin Hubble saw before anyone else the true size of Feynman's stage; not at all the naked-eye universe of our night skies, a fantastical vision, rather, of billions of galaxies each containing billions of stars, fleeing ever faster from each other in all directions. A distinguished physicist once gave me a book of his inscribed, *"To Herman Wouk, one of the few who does not write if he does not understand."* Not true here, alas. About astrophysics, I am the man on the street. As a Columbia freshman I registered for an astronomy course, but upon leafing the textbook crawling with calculus,

I dropped out fast. Astronomers, I guess, hear God talk all the time. In that language, I never will. Galileo and Newton need no further words of mine. Herewith, brief sketches of the juniors, starting with the spectacularly energetic George Ellery Hale.

Hale's father headed a major Chicago firm, Hale Elevators. His son chose stargazing over the family business, rose to distinction as a solar astronomer, declined the presidency of MIT to found and direct the Mount Wilson Observatory, coined the term *astrophysics,* and started and edited the *Astrophysical Journal,* still going strong today. With all that, building great telescopes was Hale's thing.* As Galileo worked the Medicis, so Hale worked the robber barons of the Gilded Age to build four giant tubes, each at first light the biggest on earth. Hale's first patron was Charles Yerkes, a flamboyant operator who built Chicago's streetcar system, with peculations that put him briefly behind bars. Such characters are resilient. Yerkes refurbished his image by funding Hale to erect a 40-inch refractor for the University of Chicago, "the biggest telescope in the world"—biggest by four inches.

A word about telescope dimensions. A lens *refracts* starlight, a mirror *reflects* it. The size of the primary lens or mirror dictates the size of the telescope, sometimes of the observatory. Beyond a 40-inch diameter, the weight

---

* *"The conquest of the realm of the nebulae is an achievement of great telescopes."* —*Edwin Hubble*

and color distortions of a lens make a refractor telescope impractical. In theory a mirror is practical to any size, but hard to get right. Nowadays mirrors *thirty yards* across and more are in the works, in segments controlled by computers. Edwin Hubble made his historic breakthroughs with the 60-inch and 100-inch reflectors on Mount Wilson, paid for mainly by Carnegie and a minor mogul named Hooker. The George Ellery Hale Telescope on Mount Palomar, funded wholly by Rockefeller, has a 200-inch mirror, one of the largest ever made of a single slab of solid glass. That telescope is Hale's monument, and his due. He did not live to point it toward the stars.*

Henrietta Leavitt's Donkey Work

Dick Feynman's point about the making of the atomic bomb—that it was a rabbit shoot, not a lion hunt—applies foursquare to the lifework of the junior stagehands. George Hale bagged many and varied cosmic rabbits. Henrietta Leavitt brought down only one astral quarry, but it was a lion.

The human eye is an awesome contrivance—Charles Darwin himself said that thinking about it "made his blood run cold"—but it is not up to staring for hours at

---

* *Ronald Florence,* The Perfect Machine: Building the Palomar Telescope *(New York: HarperCollins, 1995).*

one star.* Astronomy today is in good part picture taking, optical, infrared, and x-ray, and the great discoveries are found in photographic plates and spectrograms. This turn to photography late in the nineteenth century pried open the doors of Harvard Observatory to Henrietta Leavitt, a Radcliffe-educated, stone-deaf spinster. The observatory in those days was strictly men's turf, but the director, a Dr. Edward Pickering, started using ladies to do the donkey work of inspecting the men's glass plates for dots, stains, streaks, and spectra, and Leavitt joined the drudging sisterhood as a volunteer.

After some years, noting her skill, Pickering promoted her to steady employment at thirty cents an hour. She remained in that job for the rest of her life. In time he assigned to her the plates from Harvard's observatory in Peru, where the staff scanned the Southern Hemisphere skies, and in these she spotted the spoor of her lion. The meager references I've dug up about Henrietta Leavitt tend to encapsulate her find as "the period-luminosity relationship in Cepheid variables," which may not sound like much; but Michelangelo said proudly of his own work, "I have patience to get to the desired end," and Leavitt's genius was something like that, a capacity for years of anonymous eye-straining labor and analysis, to arrive at one pivotal scientific discovery.

---

* *Charles Sherrington,* Man on His Nature *(New York: Cambridge University Press, 1940).*

Cepheid variables are stars that blink. No human eye can see the blink, for it is a slow blink, and not an on-and-off blink either, just a dimming and brightening over days or weeks. The first such blinking star was discovered long ago near the North Star, in the small constellation Cepheus, hence the name. Cepheids abound in two hazy patches in the southern skies called the Magellanic Clouds, which are nearby "satellite galaxies" of the Milky Way.* Out of those southern plates, Henrietta Leavitt wrested a rigorous new truth of Nature: the slower the blink, the brighter the Cepheid. In astronomical numbers, all the Cepheids in the Magellanic Clouds were about the same distance away, so brightness varied *directly* with the duration of the blink. Therefore, if the blink was very slow, yet the star was very faint, it had to be a huge, huge distance away. She determined this to be true on a predictable scale, hence, a "period-luminosity relationship."

She then calibrated her Cepheids relative to each other, so that once some gentleman at a telescope ascertained the absolute distance of one such blinking star, her entire scale would spring to life as a major new cosmic yardstick. A Dane, Ejnar Hertzsprung, was the first to do this, and word of Leavitt's discovery rapidly spread in astronomic circles. A Swedish savant was planning to name her for a Nobel Prize, but she died of cancer at fifty-three, and

---

* For three wartime years I sailed those southern seas, stood hundreds of night watches, and never noticed the Magellanic Clouds. Alas, the astronomy course I dropped. —HW

the prizes are not awarded posthumously. Otherwise, the second female Nobel laureate in physics, after Marie Curie, might well have been Henrietta Leavitt, the deaf old maid in the Harvard shadows.

Harlow Shapley and the Great Debate

Picking up on her work, two small-town boys from Missouri, both at the Mount Wilson Observatory above Pasadena, got into a match race to measure the actual size of the universe; the goal, nothing less than recognition as the new Copernicus. Of the two, Harlow Shapley had such a head start that it seemed no contest, until Edwin Hubble galloped past him, going away.

Five years older than Hubble, Shapley arrived at Mount Wilson five years ahead of him. With access to the only 60-inch telescope in the world, this feverishly ambitious former farm boy employed and improved Leavitt's Cepheids scale to map out a new Shapley universe, year by dogged year. Hubble, meanwhile, a straight-A high-school jock who set a high-jump record, went leaping around unfocused from pursuit to pursuit. He majored in astronomy at the University of Chicago, then studied law as a Rhodes scholar at Oxford, then abandoned law for an observer's post at Yerkes, then abandoned Yerkes to volunteer for the infantry in World War I, then turned up in 1919 at Mount

Wilson, still in his army major's uniform, to start over as a junior observer.

By that time Harlow Shapley had already published almost a hundred papers and was about ready for his homestretch dash to the pantheon of science. As senior observer he had remained very much his congenial farm-boy self, putting on no airs with the staff. The newcomer by contrast had shrugged off his midwestern roots utterly; Oxford accent, austere aloofness, tweedy garb including knickers, even slang like "Bah Jove!" Shapley's oral history, compiled in his old age, tells how he judged this stuck-up young Ozarks guy with the Rhodes scholar patina "not worth much visiting with." The next year, Shapley boldly announced that he had succeeded in measuring the universe; moreover, that it was *ten times bigger* than hitherto believed. The Milky Way galaxy, encompassing all space, was 300,000 light-years across, and the Sun with its planets was not at the center, but 25,000 light-years off to a side. The world's astronomers were bowled over by his audacious conclusions, based on his privileged and indomitable work with the great 60-inch. In point of fact, Shapley's picture of the Milky Way was roughly accurate and has stood the test of time. The popular press took notice, and in his midthirties, Harlow Shapley was an international name, while Major Hubble was, so to say, left at the post.

Yet the accolades were not unanimous. A much older astronomer, one Heber Curtis, had been challenging

Shapley's journal papers all along, and Shapley had been firing back at him. George Hale, then Mount Wilson's director, sponsored a symposium at a 1920 science conference in Washington; topic, "The Size of the Universe."* Albert Einstein was there, so reporters came buzzing in for the "Great Debate," as they dubbed it. Actually the older astronomer was quite wrong, advocating an even smaller Milky Way, but he managed to trip up Shapley on an open question of the day in astronomy: the *nebulae*. Were they clumps of stardust, clouds of luminous gas (*nebulae* is Greek for "clouds"), or what? Nobody yet knew. Back in the eighteenth century, from his ivory tower in Koenigsberg, Immanuel Kant had proposed that they were "island universes" far beyond the Milky Way; just a philosopher's guess, of course, implying preposterously vast distances. But on the off chance Kant was right, what became of the Shapley universe? To Shapley the question was trivial, but it rattled him; the crusty older man drew laughs at his expense, and next day the press gave Curtis the edge.

Harvard astronomers who attended knew better. Awed by Shapley's achievement and presentation, they offered him the directorship of their observatory. He accepted the plum at a very young thirty-nine and left Mount Wilson to live out his long life at Harvard. Faint echoes of the Great Debate linger in some books on astronomy. Edwin Hubble

---

* *Richard Feynman was then two years old. I was five.* —HW

settled the matter once and for all with the new 100-inch Hooker telescope that Shapley abandoned to him. Drawing aside Shapley's low starry canopy of the Milky Way, Hubble revealed the true dark unfathomable grandeur of Feynman's Big Stage.

Hubble's Realm

Hubble's 1936 book, *The Realm of the Nebulae,* is his one try at communicating with the common reader, i.e. you and me.* At the outset he quotes with arid approval the prescient logic of Immanuel Kant; nice thinking, based on so few facts. Like Edwin Hubble himself the book is difficult to penetrate, but worth the effort in every sentence, if one will butt through the numbers, tables, and graphs. At least so I found it. Obscured by the passive voice of science journal articles, there lurks in those pages the self-portrait of a redoubtable man who knew so much, and felt himself so different, that all his adult life he assumed a persona as durable as armor, through the visor of which there may have glinted a dusky spark of proud mockery. At bottom, for sure, this was a deadly serious great scientist.

February 1924 must have been a lovely month for Major Hubble, as he was always called on Mount Wilson; not

---

* *Edwin Hubble,* The Realm of the Nebulae *(Silliman Memorial Lectures) (New York: Yale University Press, 1936).*

Dr. Hubble, and certainly never Edwin or Ned. He married far above his origins, a clever pretty widow of a socialite banking family; and in the selfsame month he was able to write Shapley that *he had found a Cepheid variable in Andromeda*. Implied was a scratch-pad result: the beautiful spiral was millions of light-years out beyond the Milky Way. On reading the letter, Shapley handed it to an aspiring female PhD in his office, saying, "This is the letter that has destroyed my universe."* Gutting Shapley's work with his own yardstick of the Cepheid variable had to be grim fun for the newlywed Major Hubble.

The 1920s were his miraculous decade, but he would not publish—possibly warned by Shapley's example—until urged to do so by colleagues. In 1925 he put out a few sparse pages dully titled "Cepheids in Spiral Nebulae," and in 1929 another laconic paper about some nebulae receding from Earth, first discerned by Slipher at a 24-inch refractor in Arizona. Stubbornly reticent, even secretive, Hubble determined, in long vigils at the 100-inch telescope, that nebulae in large numbers were not only receding but *fleeing* from Earth at velocities of thousands of miles per second; and in perhaps his finest *Aha!* moment, he discovered that the different velocities of different galaxies were on average proportional to their distances—the farther away, the faster their flight—that this was equally true of all the

---

* *Gale E. Christianson,* Edwin Hubble: Mariner of the Nebulae *(New York: Farrar, Straus and Giroux, 1995).*

receding nebulae in all directions (in science slang, "isotro-pically"), and that therefore their speeds could be calibrated as a distance-velocity relationship. This linear relationship is Hubble's Law, a new truth pulled in through the tube from outer space by the human brain, a way to find cosmic distances with a reach far, far beyond the Leavitt scale. For at those distances all the starlight in a galaxy merges as one tiny spot of light, and the spectrum of that dot yields a clue—a REDSHIFT—that gives the distance.* Measuring redshifts requires not only rare skill and acumen, but inhu-man patience like Henrietta Leavitt's. Hubble, a masterly observer, was not quite up to that. He was fortunate in a little-remembered collaborator, Milton Humason, who was in that regard Henrietta's peer.

The redshift is a Doppler effect. In antisubmarine war-fare we used Doppler all the time—echo ranging we called it—sending out sonar *pings* underwater to probe for the enemy night and day. When we made a contact and pursued it, if our *pings* that echoed back from the contact were pitched higher and higher, we were closing the bad guy; if the pitch dropped, he was getting away. Ranging on a galaxy with Doppler is more complicated, but the Old One throws in a big hint, as it were, to the groping *Homo*

---

* *Hubble stolidly used* galaxy *to mean the Milky Way only. All the others were always "extra-galactic nebulae."*

sapiens. Shoot a beam of white light through a gas, or a solid element heated to a gas, and bright lines stand out in the spectrum, always in the same place, the signature of that element. *In starlight, however, the signature lines appear black.* How comes this spectral bar code? Well, when light from (say) burning hydrogen in a star's interior passes through the cooler hydrogen at the surface, those bright lines get absorbed, leaving black gaps; and since the galaxy (bad guy) is running away—down Doppler—the bar code shifts ever so slightly lower, toward the red end of the spectrum. Milton Humason was a nonpareil fisher of these redshifts. From Hubble's preface: "The writer gratefully acknowledges an indebtedness to his colleagues at the Mount Wilson Observatory; in particular, to Milton Humason, who has contributed almost the whole of the recent data on nebular spectra and red-shifts."

Among the Mount Wilson staffers, Humason was always just "Milt," the whiskey-drinking, tobacco-chewing, poker-playing good old boy who as a teenager had driven mule teams up the mountain trails, hauling building materials for the new observatory. With only a grammar-school education, working first as a janitor at the observatory, then as a night assistant, then as a junior observer, Humason bootstrapped himself to become a leading astronomer. How he acquired Feynman's "language God talks" to make his calculations, how he learned to measure redshifts with the precision of a brain surgeon, is unclear in the books and perhaps unknowable. We know that for years on end he endured freezing nights in the dark of the moon on wind-swept Mount Wilson, photographing galaxies and taking their spectrograms to amass the rock foundation of fact on which Hubble's *Realm* stands.

Hubble and Humason

In 1931 Hubble and Humason coauthored a paper, "The Velocity-Distance Relation Among Extra-Galactic Nebulae," which made the international front pages. Albert Einstein was visiting California at the time, hounded by reporters like a movie superstar in a messy divorce. At a Caltech press conference he praised the Hubble-Humason paper as "'bringing near a presumption' that his general theory of relativity had been proven by their results." Well might Einstein casually hurl this public relations thunder-bolt, for as Galileo's discovery of Jupiter's moons backed up Copernicus, so the Hubble-Humason paper backed up Einstein. From its dense pages there rose Hubble's Law, cornerstone of the expanding-universe cosmogony, a dizzying, counterintuitive vision that the universe itself, all of space, was expanding, causing the simultaneous swelling of the distances among all the galaxies and creat-ing the optical illusion that the galaxies were accelerating away from Earth. Implicit was the origin of the universe in an ineffable primordial explosion, today accepted by most thinking men as a new Genesis, "the Big Bang," a derisive nickname that stuck, coined by a prominent astronomer who didn't believe in it at all.*

Edwin Hubble was no saint about sharing credit. All the ideas in the famous paper had been anticipated, such as by Kant on the "island universe" and by Slipher on the recession of the galaxies. It was Hubble's hard reasoning, based on the mass of Humason's observed hard facts, that welded these notions into a new cosmogony. Harlow Shapley in his book called Hubble his superior as an observer. Hubble staked his name, and his standing as a scientist, on the work of an even better observer. That was why he shared authorship of the celebrated paper with Milt, the quondam mule driver.

What Hubble did not share with Milt was his glorification triggered by Albert Einstein. Only Hubble posed for photographers with Einstein at the 100-inch telescope. Only Hubble, in a smooth transit from Pasadena to Beverly Hills, from redshift to red carpet, became chummy with Charlie Chaplin and Aldous Huxley and was made much of as only Hollywood can do it for the man of the moment. To these cynical, fiercely competitive illusion weavers, so

---

* *Sir Fred Hoyle, 1915–2001.*

quick and merciless to see through each other's preten-
sions and poses, Edwin Hubble was a six-foot-two Gary
Cooper Copernicus, with the accent and the look, even the
tweed knickers, of a Cotswold squire. They bought into
the illusion like groupies.

And why not? He had been perfecting it for decades.
Even courting his socialite inamorata, he had regaled her
family with heroic fibs; for instance, how he had agonized
over his men who fell in battle, though he had sailed across
the Atlantic and back and never heard a shot fired in anger.
They married and lived happily ever after, and for Grace
Hubble there was one and only one true great man, her
Edwin. Einstein by comparison she dismissed as "a troll,"
that is, an antic dwarf.*

Feynman sported with Las Vegas showgirls, banged on
bongo drums, picked locks at Los Alamos with boyish
glee, and taught groundbreaking physics in comedy-store
Brooklynese. Albert Einstein acted Grace Hubble's "troll"
when it suited him; one visiting colleague wrote fondly of
him, *"immer das zelber kinderskopf"*—"always the same
child mind." Stephen Hawking in our day writes and talks
through electronic devices with sly, sometimes wicked

---

* *Gale E. Christianson,* Edwin Hubble: Mariner of the Nebulae
(New York: Farrar, Straus and Giroux, 1995).

humor; in Beijing he titillated university students, telling them in his toneless artificial voice how much he liked Chinese women. Edwin Hubble's humor was to wear a mask until his born face took on that likeness. Do these rare spirits at their exalted altitudes hear a laughter in eternity—inaudible to the rest of us—that makes the Buddha smile? If so, let a groundling who once wrote jokes for a living guess at what amuses the Old One. It is *Homo sapiens,* convinced that in his Outward Bound quest he is nearing the final truth, as he runs and runs in the turning hamster wheel of eternal mystery.

Since Hubble's day the known size of the universe has doubled and redoubled, with the discovery of two types of Cepheid variables, and two types of supernovae, and quasars, and ever bigger redshifts, now nicknamed z's, so commonplace are they. A Harvard astronomer tells in a lively book, of teams of professors racing to find such ever bigger redshifts—the prize, getting there *first* with proof that the expansion of the universe is speeding up—and he remarks that the astronomers Einstein consulted in earlier days were "fogbound."* Fifty years hence astronomers yet unborn may call him fogbound; meantime it's all out to find those clinching z's first! So the hamster wheel turns and turns.

---

* *Robert P. Kirshner,* The Extravagant Universe *(Princeton, NJ: Princeton University Press, 2002).*

The Ghost Light

The play is over. The curtain falls, the houselights come up, the audience files out. In the empty theater, the curtain rises again on an unlit stage, and as the houselights go dark a stagehand brings out one bright light on a pole. He plants it center stage and departs. The naked bulb diffuses a dim glow all through the silent dark theater.

This is the Ghost Light. On heavily unionized Broadway, some call it the Equity Light. In Shakespeare's time, I'm told, the Ghost Light caused many a wooden theater to burn down. In the first instance the Ghost Light is practical, keeping people from falling and breaking their necks if they come onstage or enter the orchestra or balcony of a black-dark house. It is also there to scare off the ghosts of departed players and old plays. All empty theaters are haunted.

The theater of Richard Feynman's Big Stage is a Hippodrome vast beyond all thought, except for the handful of astrophysicists whose domain it is. No longer do they freeze on windy mountaintop observatories. At computer monitors in warm rooms, they work at varied tasks, getting digital readings from instruments far advanced since Hubble's day; instruments that may be next door or in the Canary Islands or on a peak in the Andes or orbiting in space. Some may be revising yet again Hubble's constant, the rate at which the velocities of galaxies accelerate. Hubble (and Humason) made out his constant to be some three hundred miles per second per million light-years. The new men use data from the Hubble Space Telescope to dispute Hubble on his constant; not on his law, which holds (so far) like the law of gravity.

What Ghost Light, then, illuminates this boundless theater of the Feynman Stage? Asked about religion, Richard Feynman replied with a dithyrambic paean to Nature, a sort of ad-lib agnostic Psalm, excluding from his theater a Creator who watched us struggle with good and evil, as too ridiculously petty for the venue. His words, again:

> It doesn't seem to me that this fantastically marvelous universe, this tremendous range of time and space and different kinds of animals, and all the different planets, and all these atoms with all their motions, and so on, all this complicated thing can merely be a stage so that God can watch human beings struggle for good and evil—which is the view that religion has. The stage is too big for the drama.

For Feynman, the Ghost Light was nothing but his own piercing mind, the spark of Adam in his genius brain, contemplating creation and finding it glorious but senseless. It is a popular view, also the considered view of some, not all, advanced thinkers. As for the author of this causerie, I see a different Ghost Light, distinctly there but very far off and hard to make out. It is not a single brilliant light like Feynman's intellect. It is an odd irregular flickering flame, like a tumbleweed or a low bush that has caught fire. Each time I look, there it is, burning.

CHAPTER FOUR

Homeward Bound

The Prod

So much for the Stage, now for the Drama. Conveying the true grandeur of the universe in this little book was beyond me, of course—I am no competition for the Psalmist or the Bhaghavad Gita—but Feynman's posing of the incongruity, as he perceived it, compelled an outward glance to start with, so I did my best. The Drama will be more my line, since at least I have had plays produced on Broadway.

Feynman's words, by the bye, were an extemporaneous outburst in an otherwise plodding TV interview when he was forty-one, and the Nobel Prize lay six years in the future. In those few rambling, wide-ranging, bumptious, obsessively honest lines, you have the man in full. Nor are those lines a casual blurt. He stuck to them. Introduced as "the distinguished young theoretical physicist" and then (as almost inevitable in such interviews, which I avoid as I would a plague zone) prodded about religion, he responded in character. The embarrassed station manager tried to suppress the tape and schedule another interview. In a curt letter, Feynman refused, demanding that his remarks be broadcast as recorded, since he had viewed the tape and found nothing he would change. It did go on the air, in early-morning hours when almost nobody would hear his heterodoxies, and a transcript fortunately survives.*

An esteemed fellow novelist once said he never missed a chance at sex or television. It takes all kinds. Way back when I did talk for TV or print, I was often prodded to explain how I could be pious and still succeed in such flesh-pot milieus as the novel, the theater, and the movies. Well, I am not pious, but go explain nuances to a reporter with a deadline of a thousand words by tomorrow or to a TV host with ten seconds left. It is a fair question, all the same, and serious people can probably figure out the answer for themselves. Unserious people say to me after a prod or two—at a dinner party, let's say, or a cocktail reception that I cannot get out of—"Well, I guess religion works for you, and that's okay, but it doesn't work for me." Translation: *It's nice you have that prosthetic, I'm glad I don't need it.* Variant: *I envy you, I wasn't brought up that way.*

The prosthetic inquirer is beyond reach. The variant

---

* Perfectly Reasonable Deviations from the Beaten Track: The Letters of Richard Feynman *(Cambridge, MA: Basic Books, 2005).*

inquirer interests me, and for him or her, I have written two up-front books, *This Is My God* and *The Will to Live On*. Across the years readers have let me know that those books have been engaging and useful, reward enough for such labors of love. Neither one really faces up, however, to the stark challenge posed by Feynman's commonsense prod, THE STAGE IS TOO BIG FOR THE DRAMA. Awareness of that prod has long haunted me, hence my start on this book.

The Nephew

An accomplished nephew who heads the psychiatry department at a major university once roomed in our Georgetown house for a year, when he was a hard-charging young recruit to a Nixon drug-control program. As the price of his bed and breakfast, I had him learn Talmud with me. Sharp as they come, he caught on fast to the zestful mental game, and the substance also seemed to interest him, though it did not visibly affect his man-about-town joie de vivre. Much, much time has passed. His hair is prematurely white, his winsome wife is an able trial lawyer, and their frighteningly bright twin children, boy and girl, are about to have their joint bar and bat mitzvahs, a time when parents, however brilliant and liberated, tend to think again about religion.

He made his way from Boston to my desert hermitage. After dinner I queried him avidly as usual about his field, neuroscience of the brain, for it touches on that standard catnip for philosophy majors, the mind-body problem. After that I was telling him an idea I had for a future book, when he broke in to this effect, in his old hard-charging style: "Uncle Herman, since you're asking me, let me tell you the book you *should* write. You're a unique character, and you know it. You're a total secularist in your thinking and your range of reference. It's self-evident in your writings. Friends ask me, 'What gives with that famous uncle of yours? Is he actually religious? What is that shtick? How can he be for real?' I tell them, 'Read *This Is My God,*' and if they bother, it suffices. That's not what I'm thinking about at all."

My nephew rotated the spread fingers of both hands opposite each other, as though trying to work a Rubik's Cube.

"You've fitted elements together in a way I don't grasp. *That's* what I want to understand. *That's* what you should write. I would read such a book. So would many people like me. And you're the only one to do it. You spent years in the Navy out in the South Pacific. You've spent years in and out of Hollywood, in fact you started life as a gag-man. You've spent years off and on in Israel, and you don't seem to mind the irreligion there one bit. You've endured personal tragedies that would kill some people, yet on you go in your cheerful way, to all appearances. When you were writing *The Winds of War* and *War and Remembrance,* and those two huge miniseries based on the novels, you plunged deeper into the Holocaust than anyone I know. After that how can you still believe? Or even *behave* as if you believe? How do you handle *'Where was God?'*"

Only next morning, on awakening, did it occur to me that I may now be writing the book he asked for.

Tevya and Confucius

A word about two classics important to me: *Tevya the Dairyman* and *The Analects of Confucius. Tevya* is a Yiddish taproot of my childhood, transplanted by my father from Minsk. On Broadway, of course, *Tevya* rose to glory as *Fiddler on the Roof.* Confucius I did not come to until late in life. *The Analects* is a bedside book in which I read a page or two a night, and when I reach the end I start over. It is a short book, in my paperback 170 pages, and may disappoint the curious reader as a mere Chinese *Poor Richard's Almanack.* This sacred text of a civilization that has lasted three thousand years does wear that aspect, but only to a casual glance.

Tevya's creator, Sholem Aleichem, died poor on Kelly

Street in the South Bronx, the street where my father started a storefront synagogue the year after I was born. My nephew, also a Columbia graduate, seems to wonder how my Kelly Street Jewishness could survive the college's celebrated core curriculum, a four-year total immersion in Western enlightenment. Well, Tevya survived it. It was only Broadway—sophisticated enlightened secular Broadway—that made of this old Yiddish tale an international popular musical, and of Tevya a lovable legend, embodying the worldwide clash between tradition and enlightenment. That clash is the hard truth today about the Jews, still "the smallest of peoples" as Moses called us, and about the Chinese, the largest.

Broadway welded music, humor, and dance into a work transcending orthodoxy to touch audiences in a score of languages everywhere. Tevya and his tragically vanished shtetl came back to life: quaint, funny, sad, moving, not the whole truth but true; and the Broadway magicians—composer, lyricist, librettist (an old friend), above all the master choreographer-director Jerome Robbins—were to a man liberated enlightened Jews. Jerome Robbins grew up Jerome Rabinowitz in Brooklyn, and his father came from Minsk. Sholem Aleichem was the pen name, incidentally, of Sholem Rabinowitz.

My Opening to China and Confucius

Back in 1982, I found out by chance that *The Winds of War* and *War and Remembrance* had been pirated in Red China, then a truculent closed society almost like North Korea today, though thawing a bit after the Nixon opening. The Chinese cultural attaché in Washington met my protest by contritely inviting me to visit his country with my wife, as guests of the Chinese Writers' Association. I telephoned some savvy diplomats, acquaintances on the Georgetown social circuit, about this dubious gesture of redress. "Oh, by all means go, it'll open your eyes," was the general reaction, and one old-timer said, "The street sweepers will know all about you before you get there."

So we went. On arriving in Beijing, an eye-opener straight off, sure enough: the U.S. cultural attaché informed us that the piracy had been high government policy! A team of scholars had hastily translated the books on order, with a government allotment of scarce paper for a huge popular edition, to balance the skewed Soviet account of World War II with my American historical panorama; the reason, Khrushchev and Mao had fallen out, and the communist monolith had split. The attaché brought us to meet the translators, gentle old English professors at the university, survivors of the revolution. They discussed my characters sagely, and almost offhand disclosed that China had first learned of the Holocaust through my books. Redress enough, right there!

Our taxing tour with a lively young translator ranged far and wide, red carpet all the way. We kept notes, and on coming home I dashed off an ebullient book, "China Diary." It molders away, filed somewhere in an old cabinet. My breathless account—the Great Wall, the gemlike gardens of Suzhou, the river fishermen angling with cormorants choked by iron rings, temples, pagodas, the underground tomb full of life-size clay warriors, etc.—all banal stuff; the one fresh note was the overlay of Soviet style I could recognize from my research in Russia for the two pirated novels. Tiananmen Square, for instance, seemed a massive clone of Red Square, complete with a mausoleum like Lenin's, and Mao preserved under glass for lines of the public to view. Hotel service was outright Soviet; dour matrons on each floor doling out the room keys, molasses-paced restaurant waitresses, and dreary menus of which we could eat little. For a Chinese touch, a huge thermos of hot water at night was room service.

Six years later we returned to China on the tab of the U.S. embassy. The thaw was far along. The ambassador's wife, Bette Bao Lord, author of the popular novel *Spring Moon,* had brought over *Death of a Salesman* for performance in Chinese translation, and was following it up with *The Caine Mutiny Court-Martial.* The translation obviously worked. The audiences laughed in all the right places, and watched Queeg's breakdown in an awed hush. The Beijing repertory players brought the show off smartly in U.S.

Navy gold-striped blues, and the reviews were fine. But all that is by the way.

This visit was the real eye-opener. The impassive dowdy airline stewardesses of our first trip had turned cordial and chic. In a new thirty-story Beijing hotel, the restaurant service made us blink and smile—impeccable young waiters, swiftly delivering choice fare, speaking resolute broken English with some droll mistakes, like actors in a dress rehearsal. A city on bicycles in 1982, Beijing's street scene now included much auto traffic amid the hordes of bicycles, and women pedestrians in bright dresses as well, and men in Western work clothes—no blue Mao pajamas in sight. Surprise of surprises, the Little Red Book of Mao's sayings was unobtainable! I went searching for it, Rip Van Winkle trying to get reoriented. A soiled worn copy turned up in a small tourist shop, and the man asked with a grin, handing it over to my translator, "Why does the gentleman want this?"

Liu Bayu and Wang Kuang

The most striking change was in the writers.

Back in 1982, the attaché had taken me straightaway to our hosts, the heads of the Chinese Writers' Association, though of course all knew that not they but the government had invited us. Of those five or six unsmiling Chinese in Mao garb, I surmised that two were the big boys, from their assured bearing and the deference of the others. The meeting was brief and cold. A senior novelist would climb the Great Wall with me, I was informed, and accompany us on our guided tour with a young translator. That was that. Later the attaché confirmed my guess. The tall broad-shouldered one with much the inscrutable countenance of Fu Manchu lore was Liu Bayu, presiding. The other was Wang Kuang, short and slight, editor of the Xinhua News Agency in British Hong Kong, and by rumor powerful head of the Chinese shadow government there. Returning to Beijing from the tour, we met with those two again, and they opened up a bit.

Both Liu Bayu and Wang Kuang knew of our diet laws in detail. Liu Bayu first laid on a banquet at a Buddhist restaurant. The wine flowed, and he spoke about Israel and the Jews, "cleverest people in the world." When I tried to return the compliment about the Chinese, his response was short and sharp. "No! Jews number one, Chinese number two." Wang Kuang invited us to a family-style dinner served by his daughter. The variegated dishes were all permissible, all exquisite, and Wang Kuang astonished me by discussing, as his daughter translated, Walter Scott's influence on my works.

So in 1988 I invited both to the *Court-Martial* opening. They arrived dressed like Western businessmen, in rare high spirits; and after the performance we managed a too-brief very warm reunion. When my wife and I left Beijing for Shanghai to see *Court-Martial* performed there and go home, Wang Kuang appeared unexpectedly at the train station to bid us an emotional farewell. It was years before I saw Liu Bayu again. Out of the blue, as it were, he showed up in Palm Springs, taking a day from an official touring delegation. We had not corresponded at all, yet it was an affectionate meeting as of old friends, a long lively visit of intimate talk in my garden. On an impulse I cannot quite explain, when he was taking his leave I plucked a flower and gave it to him. He accepted it gravely, his expression as inscrutable as at our first encounter, his eyes moistening.

The Analects, Book One, First Saying: *"That friends should come to one from afar, is that not after all delightful?"*

In Liu Bayu and Wang Kuang I found two sons of an ancient culture, a people keeping a hard grip on its pristine character, its *Chineseness,* in its hurtling advance to modernity. And in Confucius I find resonances with my own Jewishness: the lifelong love of learning and of teaching, the keen regard for tradition, the importance of rituals and music—bone-deep in me since Kelly Street—as essences of the Way, the good life. First Saying of the Master, Book Seven: "I have transmitted what was taught to me, without making up anything of my own." In writing about the Jewish faith I have tried to transmit, in the idiom of the core curriculum, what I have learned. Nothing more.

The Transmogrification

Still, my nephew's puzzlement at those writings is apt, for my submergence—not to say baptism—in the Enlightenment did take hold at Columbia and sank into my bones, there to battle it out for years with Kelly Street. The bell that stopped the fight was Pearl Harbor. Right up to that resounding *clang,* behold a nice religious Bronx boy living it up in an Essex House suite or some such fancy digs, a nimble wit for hire at high pay as a radio gagman, still studying the Talmud now and then with Grandpa, an amiable grace note to an otherwise free and easy lifestyle.

My transmogrification to a sleek Manhattan bon vivant began when I came to Columbia, a pudgy baby-faced freshman just turned fifteen, and latched on to the campus wit who wrote humor columns and Varsity Shows, a strong-willed upperclassman bent on writing Broadway musicals. He welcomed my boyish adulation and genially tolerated my religious foibles; son of a surgeon, graduate of a Manhattan private school, Arnold Auerbach was a "downtown Jew" with no atom of interest in that quaint stuff, except for joking about it. We made each other laugh, we spent endless hours together, and in time he helped me write my own Varsity Shows. Rudderless as I was, the old ways loosening in the Light, I seized on him for my model and guide. Straight out of Columbia we formed a gag-writing team, Arnold always top man, which prospered from the start.*

Our first employer was a Rabelaisian bear of a Jew, a brilliant Phi Bete intellectual from the Lower East Side, known as the "Gag Czar." This outrageously funny, inhumanly energetic Yiddish-speaking atheist, David Freedman, was writing for three or four comedians at the same time, and skits for Broadway revues as well, living with his large family in a plush Central Park West penthouse on nothing but a flood of hand-to-mouth earnings. In my long bildungsroman *Inside, Outside,* Freedman enters late and takes center stage as "Harry Goldhandler," a ribald pirate scrambling through headlong dodges and devices in and out of Radio City, Broadway, and Hollywood at the pace of a bedroom farce. The job was just like that, a maniacal night and day joyride, mostly hilarious, in the glamor world of quick-money showbiz. We loved the man and hung on and on until exhaustion made us quit. A year or so after we did that, the real-life "Goldhandler's" heart gave out, and he died in his sleep.

Next we were hired by the legendary Fred Allen, who

---

* *A. M. Auerbach,* Funny Men Don't Laugh *(New York: Doubleday, 1965).*

wrote his own show in a vein of dry crackling satire that won a huge audience, and devotees like John Steinbeck and James Thurber. We were "the boys," college graduate nobodies lurking in the shadow of this New England Artemus Ward, rough-drafting segments of the program to save him time. In this featherbed job we lived together for five years, collaborating—in our abundant spare time—on musical outlines nobody optioned and play ideas that didn't pan out, while pursuing our callow divergent amours. Hitler's march into Poland caught us in Cannes, disporting with the beach damsels as we drafted stuff for the new Allen season. We made it home on the last crossing of a Dutch liner before a submarine sank it.

Pearl Harbor split up the team. Arnold went into Army Special Services, where he wrote his first Broadway musical while still in uniform. I volunteered for reserve officer training in the Navy; end of the transmogrified downtown bon vivant.

The "Mutiny"

My father died when I was in midshipman school. Kelly Street took instant charge in my spirit. I went straight to the commandant and asked for a week's leave, a presumptuous, not to say insane, request in that rigidly regimented crash course. He granted it. The chaplain had picked me to run the sketchy Jewish services Friday nights, so maybe that did it.

The school was housed in a Columbia dormitory, a ten-minute walk from my parents' flat. For seven days I *"sat shiva,"* the rite of deep mourning; walked back, finished the course, and was ordered to communications school at Annapolis, and thence to a destroyer-minesweeper, USS *Zane* (DMS-14), somewhere in the South Pacific. Sailing out to war through the Golden Gate, I felt reborn, the jokewriter molting, the serious writer emerging. Somerset Maugham said in *The Summing Up* that writing a play should take about three weeks. The war would most likely last four more years, I figured, so I would write at least half a dozen plays in all that dead time. As the ungainly Liberty ship wallowed ten thousand miles over the open sea and across the equator I made a start, and with a finished play in hand, I reported aboard the *Zane,* my destination and my destiny.

Maugham also said that novelists in their books mainly write their autobiographies, and Flaubert with his famed flair for *le mot juste* put it, *"Madame Bovary, c'est moi."* When Willie Keith jumps off a teetering gangplank into the arms of the *Caine*'s officer of the deck, that is exactly how I arrived on the Zane. Tom Keefer, the disgruntled writer spinning his facile cynicisms about the Navy, and Barney Greenwald, the Jewish fighter pilot who wins the court-martial acquittal, then denounces the mutineers and Keefer the instigator, are aspects of myself, before and after four years of naval service. I learned something in those years. What I learned is what *The Caine Mutiny* is about.

Much like Willie, I shaped up through dull years of uneventful steaming under sun and stars, and bursts of wartime excitement and terror. Not in the least like Willie, I donned phylacteries, *tfilin,* and said my prayers every morning. My wardroom shipmates took that in stride, for I stood my watches, did my share of paperwork, and held up in gales and in landings under fire. Reserve officers all, landlubbers serving at sea, we rubbed along through good times and bad. For a whole year we were a disaffected lot, under a memorably bad captain who rolled not steel balls, but toothpicks. We endured, muttered, made grim jokes but no mutiny, of course, and in the crew's letters, which we had to censor, *hell ship* was a byword. As for me, I scribbled at my contrived little plays before dawn, numbly oblivious to the drama unfolding around me, which could some day make a play or better yet a novel. Indeed I had no reason to think of a novel, never having tried my hand at fiction.

The lightning struck when I read *Don Quixote.* In the long slow months of escort steaming, I was whiling away off-duty nights by working through a footlocker of the classics: Fielding, Scott, Thackeray, Dickens, and such. From boyhood on I had devoured new novels as they appeared, by remote figures like Aldous Huxley, Ernest Hemingway, Sinclair Lewis, F. Scott Fitzgerald, nothing to do with me or my aspirations. Coming on Cervantes' book—the fountainhead of novels old and new—in the footlocker, I suddenly saw the novel as something I could try to do myself! My fourth play, *Aurora Dawn,* was well along, but I started it over as a book from page one.

Once there was a bright and spirited young man named Andrew Reale...

Aurora Dawn

I was like one set free. No more groping for dialogue, exits, entrances, curtains, and curtain lines! The plot of the play rolled out smoothly *as a story.* For a style, on a brash impulse, I was trying on the mock-heroic irony of Fielding. The characters seemed to be coming to life under my hand, the scenes to be really happening. For months I scrawled and scrawled away, having marvelous fun piling up yellow pages in snatched wee morning hours. After writing four chapters I froze, like a rock climber losing his nerve and clinging to the cliff's face for dear life. Was I *crazy?* What the hell was I doing, attempting a *NOVEL?* My enthusiasm died, my motivation shriveled. I sent a typed copy of my scrawls to my mentor, the Columbia philosophy professor Irwin Edman, as I had done with three footling plays which had not impressed him at all.

Half a year of war dragged by. I was ordered to another DMS, the *Southard,* as executive officer. One morning in

May 1945, a mailboat delivered to the *Southard* off Okinawa a mildewed sack of long-delayed correspondence.
Amid my true love's many letters arrived a total surprise,
a frenzied communication from a clerk at the Columbia
bookstore who doubled as a minor literary agent. The
woman had shifted her typewriter ribbon to whoop in red,
"SUCCESS! Simon and Schuster have taken your book!!!"
Irwin Edman, bless his photographic memory—*Aurora
Dawn* is dedicated to him—had quoted early pages verba-
tim to an editor at lunch. The editor had taken the bait and
asked to read the script. Irwin's reassurance from peaceful
Philosophy Hall came halfway around the world, faint but
clear: *"You're not crazy, this can work, keep going."*

We took a kamikaze around then, which luckily missed,
hitting the sea off our bow. As exec of a ship in hazard I
had no time even to look at my scrawls. When the atomic
bomb ended the war I became even busier in the transit
to peacetime, the quickened turnover of the crew, and the
onset of the typhoon season. Okinawa was hit twice. The
second blow drove the *Southard* up on rocks that punctured
the old hull. A harbor boat got us all safely off the wreck,
and once we were lodged aboard a transport full of other
typhoon survivors, I had nothing but time. Out came the
yellow sheets from the *Southard*'s mail pouch in which I
had rescued them, and by the time I went on inactive duty,
married my true love, and got her pregnant, *Aurora Dawn*

was more than half written, and I no longer doubted my calling. I was the new Henry Fielding.

The book got a drubbing in prominent places—rite of passage—and some plaudits by lesser reviewers; the one good word from an important critic, a friend of Irwin's, was, "a nice talent for light fiction." Right on. *Aurora Dawn* is a sketch of my Fred Allen days, a spoof of the radio advertising game livened with some Navy characters, and not a Jew in sight. This "specious stunt," as I later called it in my diary, is still in print after sixty years, a pretty slow start toward *The Winds of War* and *War and Remembrance,* but a start.

The Mavericks

Deep in the archives of Caltech, a peculiar artifact of Richard Feynman's career long lay buried, a transcript of his three 1963 Danz Lectures at the University of Washington. Flashes of his razor-edged intellect shone through the extemporaneous rambling, but taken as a whole the document verged on self-caricature, so it struck me when with some difficulty I dug it out; a hundred pages of the bongo-drumming impish Feynman dubbed by a fellow theorist "the Elvis Presley of science." The third lecture especially seemed an exercise in time killing. He set up straw men—believers in UFOs, astrology, and systems to beat roulette—then shredded them with the rough sarcasm of an arguer in a bar; or he flogged dead horses like television commercials, insincere politicians, and dumbbell interviewers. Sir Francis Crick fashioned his Danz Lectures into a book, *Of Molecules and Men,* and Feynman's lectures have recently been brought out as a book titled *The Meaning of It All.**

Early in the first lecture, where he deals with science as it relates to religion, Richard Feynman does come close to articulating an earnest personal faith, in his unbuttoned diction and stand-up comedy style; a creed much like the humanism I imbibed at Columbia, as set forth by the avatar of the core curriculum, Irwin Edman, in his *Philosopher's Quest.* Feynman never once mentions humanism, and another word he never mentions is *Judaism.* Now consider: here is a man whose father like mine emigrated from Minsk and like my father—and so many immigrant Jewish fathers—wore out his life and sharp mind in a small business, to give his children an education and their shot at American careers; whose father like mine died young and like mine had a Jewish burial. Melville Feynman was an avowed atheist who now and then attended a temple, and once got his famous son to give a talk there on the atomic bomb. At his father's interment Feynman icily declined to

---

* *Cambridge, MA: Basic Books, 1998.*

repeat the Kaddish in Hebrew or English, as in boyhood he had balked at having a bar mitzvah. Not a trace of that Jewish background is in those hundred pages. Where it might naturally emerge, Feynman pirouettes on humanist toes around a void.

All the same, he and I had a lot in common. For one thing, when we strolled and talked in Aspen, he spoke of his meagerly educated father with deep insight and admiration; only late in life, truth to tell, have I come to understand my own father in such depth. We were both mavericks, and narrow-gauge mavericks at that; Feynman with his street-smart style of teaching science, I with my plain narrative voice bucking the modernist and postmodernist tides. Just as I did not know calculus, so Feynman had no knowledge of fiction. Novels did not interest him, he told me, because made-up stories could not compare to the ever-exciting surprises of nature. Indeed when we first met at Caltech, as the reader may recall, he said my planned novel about the global war was *the kind of thing genius reaches out for,* whereas at the time anyone in the know about serious fiction would have snapped, "Are you out of your bloody *mind?* Historical romance is middlebrow dead mackerel!" *The Winds of War* and *War and Remembrance,* appearing one by one over fourteen years, found a broad and durable international audience; as the Feynman Diagrams, his offbeat pictorial handling of equations in electrodynamics, took hold worldwide as a popular tool.

The Humanists

In the late Sir Francis Crick, Feynman had a stern fellow humanist. Molecular biology, Crick asserted in his Danz Lectures and again in *Molecules and Men,* was killing "vitalism" stone dead, by accounting for all life in terms of chemistry and physics.* When Napoleon commented that the Marquis de Laplace's great book, *The System of the World,* left out God, Laplace stiffly rejoined, "I have no need for that hypothesis," and Sir Francis felt that way about vitalism, taking it as a veiled vestige of religion in science best stamped out.

It was Crick and James Watson, of course, who in 1953 "found the secret of life," as they publicly exulted, by unraveling the huge marvelous molecule DNA, *deoxyribonucleic acid,* which governs the structures of plants, bacteria, mice, elephants, you and me, in short, of all living things. Every couch potato knows about DNA as a hot crime-scene clue, also as the giveaway of a baby's father, but it is difficult stuff to get a real handle on. I keep reading books on biology. The flood of recent discoveries is overwhelming, and my grasp of the science remains akin to my halt at calculus in physics. Once I heard Richard Feynman, in a television interview, put down biology as a soft science compared to

---

* Vitalism: *a doctrine that the processes of life are not explicable by the laws of physics and chemistry alone. —Henri Bergson*

physics. I quoted this to an old friend, a leading British geneticist. He sagely commented, "What Dick Feynman needs is a swift kick in the arse." Vitalism, incidentally, is dropping from sight these days, done in as much by fashion as by molecular biology. Philosophy has its trends, like hairdos.

Not long after Crick and Watson won their Nobel laurels, a team of Bell Lab scientists earned a Nobel for a discovery as cardinal as DNA, and a lot simpler to understand. These two radio astronomers, Arno Penzias and Robert Wilson, scanning the skies as usual, happened on a very weak inexplicable signal coming from all directions—*isotropic* is the jargon term—that wasn't a glitch in their instruments, for they checked, and checked, and rechecked. With the glorious *AHA!* of a scientific lifetime, they realized *they had found the cosmic microwave background radiation.* This faint residual radiant heat fits into Edwin Hubble's theory of an expanding universe the way a plug fits a socket. As the galaxies flee ever deeper and faster into space, their redshifts give their speed, acceleration, and distance by Hubble's Law. Astrophysics reverses the numbers, runs them backwards in time, and arrives at a point in cosmic history some fifteen billion years ago, when the universe, in an instantaneous cataclysm of radiation and heat, was THERE. A microwave trace of that radiant heat was predicted to linger everywhere in the cosmos. *That* was the Bell team's strange isotropic buzz, and with this confirmation of Hubble's theory, the big bang blazed forth in cosmology and in popular belief.

If DNA solves the prime secret of life, that radiation solves the prime secret of the universe: *Is it eternal, without a beginning or an end in time, or did an origin out of nothing once occur?* Unlike the ancient Jews, who had their pat Mosaic answer in Genesis, the Greek thinkers sought an answer to the riddle in nature, based on human reasoning. Such speculation, then as now, disturbed the prevailing religion. The 1920s monkey trial in Tennessee was foreshadowed more than two millennia earlier by the trial of Socrates in Athens. The old philosopher, condemned to die for teaching disbelief in the gods, denied the charge but serenely quaffed the fatal hemlock and faded from life, so Plato writes, cheering up the grieving disciples around his couch to the last.

Is there a hint, in the cosmic microwave background radiation, that a Creator, the unnecessary hypothesis of Laplace and Crick, may be astir after all? Rabid humanists and rabid believers may agree on nothing else, but on this one thing they now agree. There was a Beginning. It happened.

The Two Dramas

The curtain rises on the Mosaic drama, and LIGHT floods the stage; on the humanist drama, a BANG shakes the theater. Beyond those two mighty metaphors, calculated to shock our primal human senses, the scenarios diverge. The old drama, starting with Adam and Eve in the Garden, still plays to about half the human race: the Christians, the Muslims, and the handful of us Jews. The new drama plays mainly to the university-educated few in the West (including me) and to an Asian elite who are making a mark of late in science and technology. How they reconcile their advanced thinking with their ancient traditions is not in my range to tell. It does fall to me, at this juncture, to tell how the life I have led, and the works I have written, square with the old-time religion; how, in rigorous honesty, I can manage to fit the two dramas together. A tall order! To arrive at private convictions and live by them is one thing, to put them into print for all to see and weigh and prod is quite another.

That scuffed old file in my workshop, *A Child's Garden of God,* contains pages dating back to the 1960s, when I decided to annoy an eminent Harvard professor, I. Bernard Cohen, by consulting him about *my* foggy vision of a book on this theme.* He no doubt wondered, when he got my letter, what the devil I wanted of him, but *The Caine Mutiny* is a good calling card, so he welcomed me to visit him at his home in Cambridge. At first when we met I hemmed and

---

* *I. Bernard Cohen is the author of* The Newtonian Revolution *(New York: Cambridge University Press, 1983). Cohen taught History of Science at Harvard for sixty years.*

hawed, then at last burst forth with a tirade about a book I meant to write, showing that science and our Jewish Bible needn't in truth clash, that the mysterious universe and our miraculous little planet alike showed a Purpose and a Hand, an ill-informed passionate outpouring that surprised even me as I heard myself deliver it. I must have gone on for fifteen or twenty minutes. The professor's puzzled attitude altered to a round-eyed attentive stare. He said when I stopped, all talked out, "Wow, big," and let it go at that.

Next day we had lunch in a fish restaurant. "Of course I don't agree with you, I think it's all stochastic," he told me. "Still, I'd be interested to see how you do it." I asked whether I should try to bone up on the science. He shook his head. "You're fifty years too late. Write down what you told me." With this reaction of an academic whose works I much admired, I had my first inkling that *A Child's Garden of God* might not be just one more brainstorm best left in the file. I have still to prove otherwise, of course, as I creep ahead into this minefield on my lame paws.

Years later I joined a Caltech excursion to Hawaii to watch a total eclipse of the Sun. There I encountered Harold Zirin, head of Caltech's solar observatory, whose affable Jewish warmth led me to ask whether I could talk to him someday about a book I had in mind. "Any time," Hal said. More years went by before I phoned him for a meeting. He remembered, and we agreed to have lunch at the Atheneum, where gourmet food and wine relieve the austerity of Caltech's brainy pursuits. He was waiting there with a colleague, a startling surprise, for this was the world-known Dutch astronomer Maarten Schmidt, who discovered the quasar with the Hale telescope.

At table with this formidable duo, I ran on and on about the book, of which I had not yet written a word. Harold Zirin heard me out with a small genial smile, halfway between approval and amusement. Maarten Schmidt's look as he listened was distant, serious, intensely concentrated, as though peering through the Hale at a possible supernova. Harold then spoke up, a wise Jew who knew just where he stood on his Judaism, didn't agree with me in the least, but had enjoyed hearing me talk about my planned quixotic sally. Schmidt's laconic comment became my mantra for writing the book: "It can be done," he said slowly and pensively, "but it is very, very hard."

Curtain Up

He has made everything beautiful in its time
and has put the universe in their hearts, except
that a man will not find the work that the Lord
has wrought from beginning to end.

ECCLESIASTES 3:11

The Hebrew root word for the universe, OLAM, takes in not only all Space but all Time, and it can mean this world as well, our beautiful little Australia in space, which has been circling the Sun, so we have learned, for some three or four billion years. Richard Feynman's biographer chose one of his many quoted sayings as the epigraph for his whole life story: *"I was born not knowing and have only had a little time to change that here and there."** Call that a humble humanist scrawl in the margin of Ecclesiastes by a melancholy Jewish genius, whose humor it was to sport the persona of a raffish bongo drummer.

Curtain up on the Humanist Drama.

---

* *James Gleick*, Genius: The Life and Science of Richard Feynman (*New York: Vintage, 1993*).

CHAPTER FIVE

Home

The Peers

BANG!!!!

It happens with no noise, of course. No ears to hear, no medium to carry sound waves. Nobelist Steven Weinberg—we met him in our opening chapter—wrote the best book I know of on the big bang, *The First Three Minutes;* 150 pages of large print, no equations. Only his peers in astrophysics, three or four thousand living souls out of all mankind, can tell whether Weinberg's book really measures up to his bold catchy title. The rest of us believe what he writes, not for his clarity, nor for his tone of authority, but because we rely on those peers to judge him worthy of our belief. Such unnamed peers are key to this whole chapter. When we get to human history I'll stand on my portraits of human nature in my books, and the handling of politics and war in the panoramic novels about World War II and Israel. About science I know less than the science editors of your favorite newspaper or website, who also lean on the peer elite in reporting new discoveries. The peers are too busy making the discoveries, unless they generously take time to write books like *The First Three Minutes*.

In Aspen, Feynman and I had a brief exchange about peers. Most of the time he did the talking, which entirely suited me. Years earlier in our meeting at Caltech he had said, "While you're talking, you're not learning anything," and I was avid to learn everything I could from this man. One day as we munched our sandwiches in a local cafeteria, he asked me what I was working on. I told him I was writing a Battle of Midway passage in my still-unnamed sequel to *The Winds of War,* which was then out in paperback after a long lodgment as a *New York Times* #1 bestseller. Feynman hadn't heard of *The Winds of War* and inquired how it had gone. I recounted its success and also its disappointing critical reception, which, shading things a bit, I declared I had taken lightly. "Ah, well, a man wants the praise of his peers," he observed with a slight smile, and went on with his explication of the classic two-slit experiment in quantum mechanics, crystal-clear as he told it, damnably slippery ever since.

Feynman's offhand remark brought me up short. Back then in the seventies, I was your touchy popular author to the life. Frivolous irresponsible reviews were mosquito bites that faded, but there had been heavyweight derogation, too. George Orwell writes in his essay "Inside the Whale" that survival is the first test of any work of art, and that is true enough; but when a novel comes off the press that verdict is thirty years off, not at hand to soothe hurt vanity. Ernest Hemingway claimed he was the most lambasted of living novelists, and he probably could have proved it. Critics who matter do not jump all over inconsequential work. The lambasters, however, were not Hemingway's peers. The eminent Victorian literary critic, George Henry Lewes, dismissed Dickens as an unserious author, with a knack for "hallucinatory" vividness. The big serious author of the day, Mary Ann Evans—pen name George Eliot—was George Lewes' mistress. As my old friend Kurt Vonnegut was wont to say, "So it goes."

But so it does not go in science. Science has peer review, a controlling structure of eminent equals, who police the integrity and merit of each other and of new work as it is published.

The Scorned

Ah, well, but the peers can flub it, too. At a summer retreat a few years ago I met an amiable man with a clever youthful face, oddly framed in a cloud of curly white hair. We sat down side by side at a rustic table where a number of men ate lunch together, and he told me he worked on mad cow disease. An old gent opposite us quizzed me on my books, then pumped him about his ailing bovines. As he answered question after question, I said to myself, stunned, "Why, this son of a bitch is talking Nobel Prize," and I said as much aloud, edited. Well, yes, Stanley Prusiner confirmed, he had received the award for discovering a protein he had named the *prion,* which infected nervous system and brain, killing not only cows, but sheep with a plague called scrapie, and human beings with the rare Creutzfeldt-Jakob disease.

Prusiner's Nobel lecture is not without a bitter aftertaste of the scorn he endured. The house of neuroscience fell in on him. His peers were desperately trying to find a virus that caused mad cow disease, and his assertion of a *protein* as the agent was unheard of and infuriating. Prusiner is one of the few scientists in his field who in recent years have won solo awards. Another was the botanist Barbara McClintock, who made major discoveries in the genetics of maize plants, building on Mendel's work with peas. She also was overwhelmed by ridicule of her findings— and of her gender as well—until she stopped publishing altogether and went on with her work in anonymity. In her old age her results emerged from long eclipse into recognition, whereupon she was overwhelmed with awards and honors. The wheels of the peer system grind slowly, but they ground out at last for both Nobelists their due, because science has an arbiter whose word is unchallengeable law; called in the humanist drama Nature, and in the old, of course, the Creator.

Literature has no such last word. Even time's verdict remains moot. T. S. Eliot wrote groundbreaking modernist poetry, and as a literary critic his stature was magisterial. In an essay on Shakespeare he declared *Hamlet* a failure, and *Coriolanus* his best play. Vladimir Nabokov pronounced Dostoevski a plaster idol begging for a demolition hammer. Who is to say they were wrong? Tomorrow you may learn in some serious review journal or smart magazine that Mark Twain was a clown of his time, no longer readable. In science the delay may be long, but the Arbiter speaks at last.

I write in this chapter what I have learned from the peers, who have learned what they know by putting to the Arbiter meticulously correct questions and getting infallible answers. Bernard Cohen advised me not to bone up on science, so if the peers have been wrong, I will be wrong. I have faith in them, or should I rather say, in their method, the method of Galileo, Bacon, and Newton, of observation, number, and measure now known as science, which has transformed the life of man for the better, if with scary risks of terminal folly.

The Missing Link

After Weinberg's three minutes nothing much happens in the humanist drama for some eleven billion years. Yes, the curtain goes up, but until human beings struggle for good and evil, which is Richard Feynman's definition of the drama, there ensues the mother of all stage waits. No "begats" to bridge the stage waits and get to exciting scenes like the Flood and the Tower of Babel, nothing but conjectural astrophysics and chemistry, fiery radiant whirling visions for mind-numbing ages. Then come cosmology, geology, paleontology, eras, periods, epochs, the whole vast net of human wit cast backward by the peers far out into the abysmal ocean of the past, from their narrow rocky shore of the Holocene; the present day, that is. With that net grand truths have been hauled in, to the glory and the humbling of the creature we are, *Homo sapiens*.

Far, far back in the net—yet much closer to us than to Weinberg's first three minutes—Lucy was caught, the first player in the scenario, a fossilized female found in northern Ethiopia in 1974. Lucy lived some three to four million years ago, she appears to have walked upright, she was taller than a chimpanzee but nowhere near our size, and her bones show similarities to the skeletons of both species. The crown jewel of Ethiopia's prehistory, jealously prized by the government, Lucy will soon tour the United States for a few years on Texas money, starting in Houston.

A newspaper phrase of my childhood, *"the missing link,"* undeniably denotes Lucy's fascination. When the monkey trial was going on in Tennessee, I was a Bronx boy of ten, a Yankees fan, and I followed the trial as avidly as I did Babe Ruth's home runs. "The missing link" was a hot news story, with lurid representations of Java Man, Peking Man, and Piltdown Man, ugly hairy glaring Calibans. Even the funnies joked about the missing link. That trial did more for Charles Darwin than all the disputation between scientists and religious believers since he published *The Origin of Species,* the difficult tome that started the trouble. The trial made him a household name, and his theory common coin, whether in one's view it came up heads for the Bible or tails for the monkey.

From Lucy, of course, it is a long, long pull to the paleontologists who dug her up, calculated her age, and detected in her skeleton some match-ups to the bones of both chimps and paleontologists. To call her a player is sort of a stretch, maybe, because the hominids—so the peers term fossils like Lucy—march through aeons of geologic time before Lucy and millions of years after her. Not until half a million years ago do they start using fire, and the jump to the burial sites and simple stone tools of the Neanderthals takes another few hundred thousand years. How can we be sure that all this is so? The skull of Piltdown Man, it turned out, was adroitly faked with a human cranium and an ape's jawbone, yet it hocused all the peers in paleontology for forty years. Well, the field has much advanced since then. Lucy's age has been arrived at by chemical analysis of the sediments where she slept. Chemistry is rock-hard science. The Texans can pretty nearly rely on the peers that she is the genuine article.

Beguiled by Lucy, I am running ahead of the humanist drama I undertook to sketch. *Cherchez la femme,* sure, but the play requires a setting as well as a stage, so a word first about the mise-en-scène, before we come to human beings struggling with good and evil.

The Raft

"Spaceship Earth," once a striking metaphor for man's place in the cosmos, today is a Disney World attraction. Not only is the metaphor too threadbare for our humanist drama, it is altogether wrong, for it implies *design,* and I. Bernard Cohen put the humanist view in the fewest, best words, "I think it's all stochastic." A spaceship is the reverse of stochastic. It is a pinnacle of design, pure design, a clever complex structure wholly man-made—which in the agnostic outlook is precisely what religion is, too.

Mark Twain in book after book poured funny agnostic scorn on religion, which much entertained me in boyhood; and in *Huckleberry Finn,* he created the image I will borrow for the setting of Feynman's drama. Maybe this image was part of Twain's vision for his book, maybe it wasn't, but it has occurred to me, and I'll stay with it. I say that this mote in the universe on which we pass our lives—only eight thousand laughable miles from pole to pole, forever rotating like a tilted gyroscope with nothing holding it up, and circling a nothing yellow star amid billions and trillions of stars, boundless light-years off in all directions— this Earth of ours, I say, is a lot more like the crude raft Huck and Jim snag to ride down a randomly winding river, than like the newest manned spacecraft still on NASA's drawing boards.

The raft image has peculiar resonance, moreover, for the humanist mise-en-scène. As a sixth-grader I noticed, in the world map hung on the schoolroom wall, that South America and Africa could fit together almost like jigsaw pieces. Class show-off that I was, I yearned for the teacher to throw me a cue to spring up and point this out. She never did, and no wonder. Not until about twenty years ago was the preposterous notion accepted that all the continents once fitted together in a single landmass, that they came apart, and that they now drift about on colossal "plates," called *raftlike* in my grandson's college textbook of geophysics.* A British geographer, Mackinder, first proposed this brainstorm in 1904, in an article that his peers ignored. In 1915 Wegener, a German meteorologist, published *Origins of Continents*

---

* *Frank Press and Raymond Siever,* Earth, *Fourth Edition (New York: W. H. Freeman and Co., 1985).*

and Oceans, a book citing much hard evidence from geology and paleontology, to support his theory of a primordial supercontinent, PANGAEA, that broke apart into moving plates. With a world war on, the book went unnoticed, but once translations appeared in 1923, the peers of earth science pounced on Wegener and gave him and his ludicrous "Pangaea" a full-throated academic howling down.

Unlike Prusiner and McClintock, Wegener never lived to savor his vindication. His pioneer weather studies took him time and again on expeditions into the harshest wastes of northern Greenland; and there, attempting to rescue colleagues stranded on the ice, he perished. As the decades wore on, advancing technology threw so many hints that Wegener had guessed right—seafloor spreading, rock upwellings, seismic waves, magnetic field reversals—that at last the exploring geophysicists submitted to the Arbiter's ruling, bought into Wegener's theory, "Pangaea" and all, and conferred respectability on it as *plate tectonics.* In the sixth grade today children learn about Pangaea and plate tectonics as truth like the Earth's rotation, and the teacher points out on the world map how South America and Africa obviously fit together like jigsaw pieces.

In the realm of higher learning, however, the peers still ponder a hole in Wegener's theory, about which he ruefully wrote that another Newton would have to arise to close it: to wit, what monster force exists on this small planet that could possibly pry the continents apart and keep the plates moving? The short answer is, the peers don't know. Their best guess: the terrestrial globe is a kind of heat engine, the monster force is geothermal energy built up over the four billion years of the planet's existence; the main heat source is the trace of radioactive elements, chiefly uranium, in the deep mantle of heated rock between the tenuous crust and the presumed molten iron core; very slow convection might have occurred over geologic time in that mantle, and...

And more than enough! The house I have lived in for many years sits plumb on the notorious San Andreas Fault; earthquakes have shaken me to my bones, hence my going on and on about plate tectonics and those sliding, colliding continental rafts, in which I am a true believer. We all know, here in Palm Springs, that the Big One is coming. The only question is—*when?* Each of us quietly hopes, "Not in my time." In that respect, if in few others, a nonagenarian has it over the other folks.

Our drama, then, takes place on a raft carrying us down a river; carrying us, what's more, *at the speed of light!* When I first heard a lecturing astrophysicist toss off that assertion I couldn't believe my ears, so first chance I got, I asked another astrophysicist, easily his peer and a good friend of mine, what the devil the man had meant. "Well, yes," said my friend with some reluctance, "that is formally true, but the continuum of spacetime matters mainly in gravitational theory on a cosmic scale, or down in the subworld of quantum mechanics."

Shaking my old head, I turn to our workaday mise-en-scène, our little global raft drifting nowhere in particular in space or spacetime.

The Small Bang

One and only one event compares to the big bang in this drama. A few chemicals, out of the ninety-two found in Nature, once coalesced on our raft and detonated (or by humanist dogma, evolved) into a peculiar creature; a creature who looked up from hunting and gathering food to watch the blinding, blazing hot ball overhead slowly cross the blue dome and sink out of sight; watched the dome fade to black with spangles of light and observed how a paler ball would cross the black dome, a changeable shape that would gradually shrink to a sliver and swell back to a ball; observed that these things occurred in exactly the same way over and over and over—*and the creature wondered and was awed.* That was the SMALL BANG, the universe giving birth to a mind—the only one we know about, so far—which in time could grasp that the big bang had happened, and could trace it all the way back to its first three minutes. Professor Diamond in *The Third Chimpanzee* calls this development the Great Leap Forward, dates it back to about fifty thousand years ago, and ascribes it, not without a touch of perplexity, to the slight difference—only

1.6 percent—between the DNA of *Homo sapiens* and his two fellow chimpanzees.

Greater men have known that perplexity. Sir Francis Crick acknowledged that *consciousness* remains an anomaly in molecular biology, a hard nut that his field has yet to crack; and Darwin himself confessed bemusement at the mystery of man's awareness of the past and the future, uniquely among the animals from which he descends. For only about fifty thousand years, at any rate, has the creature *Homo sapiens* been struggling with good and evil, while achieving dominion over the other creatures. The fossil record shows that dinosaurs—Greek for "terrifying lizards"—dominated Pangaea for something like a *quarter of a billion years*. Surely that protracted lizard prologue to our eyeblink humanist drama should give pause to the thoughtful reader. What, nothing left of those aeons upon aeons of wasted time but huge horrid long-toothed skeletons in museums and a bit of nightmarish fun in Hollywood blockbusters? Has it really all been such a vastly drawn-out complex purposeless nonsense?

I'll venture that not even a solid savant like Steven Weinberg can believe that, not in his innermost soul. What he can do is turn his face up and hurl defiance at the cosmos: *"Yes, I observe. Yes, I wonder. Yes, I am awed. But not by you, for on the available evidence, you are not there. Why I am here, I cannot tell; why it has all happened this way, dinosaurs and all, I cannot begin to tell; and if I be damned, I be damned."* In the raft story, Huck Finn arrives at the same defiant readiness to be damned, though unlike the savant, he dreads (in his words) the "One that's always on the lookout." He dreads too the name of *abolitionist;* abhorrence of such nigger-loving agitators is in his blood, breathed in with his native air. Yet he opts to incur that disgrace and hellfire, for the sake of his chum on the raft, a runaway black slave.

Mark Twain was five years in his grave when I was born. About that time a door-to-door book salesman, canvassing the Jewish Bronx, sold my mother a set of the complete works of "the American Sholem Aleichem." One Friday night some ten years later, I brought a book from that set into the dining room, where my parents still sat at the candlelit table after dinner. On Friday night my father often read to us from Sholem Aleichem, but on this night I read to them, laughing and gasping till the tears came, a scene from *Huckleberry Finn.* They exchanged a look. The American Sholem Aleichem was getting through to their boy! I still have that green-bound volume, rat-gnawed and falling apart. Leafing its yellowed pages, I marvel that in our largely Yiddish-speaking household, I could follow Huck's southern lingo at all, yet I sure did, devouring that book time and again, best story I had ever read, lots of great adventures, some funny, some sad; and when Huck decided to defy God and his upbringing to steal Miz Watson's nigger Jim out of a lockup, saying to himself, *"All right, then, I'll go to hell,"* I wanted to cheer.

Call *Huckleberry Finn* Twain's masked Civil War novel on the theme that the cause of the South was wicked and doomed, and its zest for war as romantic Walter Scott adventure—Twain's own boyhood fantasy—a fatal mistake. Of military age when the war began, young Sam Clemens of Hannibal, Missouri, lit out for the Nevada territory and took no part in the fight for black slavery; so we have no big bowwow war novels by Samuel Langhorne Clemens, only the collected works of Mark Twain.

Twain labored for seven years off and on to produce a sequel to *Tom Sawyer,* taking the bizarre artistic liberty that Huck himself wrote the book. In *Tevya,* the simple dairyman told his story to Sholem Aleichem, who merely recorded his words; a stretch, but tolerable literary license. It was wildly ridiculous, however, to pretend that a vagrant river boy could compose this uproarious, tragic, slapstick odyssey, as layered with meanings as an ancient epic poem. How was it, then, that in a fifth-floor Bronx tenement flat, I was reached and held spellbound by the voice of that boy, in truth the ventriloquist voice of a dead and buried literary giant? It happened because Twain, with a seven-league stride of genius, went and diverted the broad river of English prose into a free-running American stream, murmuring a clear new music that a sixth-grader son of immigrant Russian Jews could hear. *Art*—above all the art of writing—was the true great leap forward of the small bang.

The Bony Girl

Framed on the wall of my small workshop is a Chinese ideogram more than a foot high, meaning "Long Life"; one thick brush stroke black on white, a gift of the calligrapher, wife of the Beijing writer who was our tour guide in 1982. And here I am in 2007, racing the calendar to finish this simple causerie and get on to the next book. The Talmud admonishes, *"Take nobody's blessing lightly."* A well-known physicist I read about had a horseshoe nailed up over the door to his lab, stoutly denied being superstitious, and when asked by his peers why, in that case, the horseshoe was there, he replied, "Well, it works." That is sort of how I feel about that ideogram.

When we returned to China in the late 1980s, I bought a paperback beforehand, a sort of *Chinese for Dummies,* figuring to learn how to read menus and street signs at least. The effort gave me a dusky glimpse into an intellectual tool of striking subtlety, breadth, and beauty, though as to menus and street signs, I weakened. The Chinese seem to have multiplied pictures upon pictures to create their written language, instead of reducing pictures to a few stylized symbols, as in most ancient alphabets. I got an inkling of the scope of their script when a youngish American journalist with a Karl Marx beard invited me to his Beijing apartment. His wife, a beautiful taciturn Chinese, gave me a sweet smile, a modest "Hello," and sat mum as he and I chatted, while a lively bony daughter of eight or so skylarked around, taking in every word and shooting us impish glances. All at once the girl grabbed pen and paper and did a quick villainous caricature of me. "Look at her," said the father fondly, as she handed me the sketch and skittered away, "she lives in two worlds and has to master both. She'll do it too, and for starters, poor kid, she'll have to learn five thousand Chinese characters." Up spoke the wife, "*Ten* thousand," a peremptory snap.

That bony girl would today be in her thirties, with any luck as seductive as her mother, and surely smart like both parents. She would have mastered those ten thousand characters with ease; and as for our Roman alphabet—the code to all Western literature, history, and culture, a mere twenty-six characters—duck soup. Yet that alphabet may have been one way the West got the drop on China. Marco Polo found in the Far East a high alien culture ruling a huge empire, powerful in warfare, behind Europe in some aspects, ahead in others. For sure, China had gunpowder first. How was it, then, that in a few centuries this two-thousand-year imperium was brought down by the armed forces of Europe? Well, for one thing, the nations crowding that crooked little peninsula of Eurasia shared the Roman alphabet, with access to the lore of Egypt, Greece, and Judea, and the formidable heritage of ruined Rome, and the science and technology of the Renaissance. An overpowering edge, while it lasted! The British gave the coup de grâce to Old China with the unprovoked assault of the Opium Wars, and the cycle of dynasties collapsed forever. It is an obscure, ill-taught historical key to what is happening nowadays.

The Inca civilization, by contrast, had no written language; their means of ruling, communicating, and doing business remain a puzzle to scholars today. A band of steel-clad European bravos on horses smashed Inca society overnight, and the priests coming on their heels to baptize the heathens wrote down what little we know of Inca history. The Incas never recovered. The Chinese, with a written language older than Rome's, came back strong. "Let China sleep," said Napoleon. "When she wakes, Europe will be sorry." Europe and America—the West's last chance on a new continent—rudely shook China awake, and a new great game is on, this time for world stakes.

Before I left that journalist's apartment, the doting parents asked me to sign and date the caricature for the bony girl as a keepsake, also to autograph for her their worn blue-bound Chinese translation of *The Winds of War*. Perhaps, all grown up now, she still has those mementos and may have read my novel, either in the columns of ideograms on the coarse gray paper of Maoist times, or in a current American paperback to hone her English. Either way she would have heard again, unchanged by time and distance, the voice of the visitor she mocked in girlish frolic so long ago; even as in boyhood I heard a far greater voice speak from the beyond on the same wondrous wavelength, the art of writing.

Invariance

Richard Feynman had no bar mitzvah. As his biographer puts it, "The gentle hearth-centered Reform Judaism of his parents left him cold...the whole pastel mosaic of holiday legends and morality offered to Jewish children on Sunday mixed fiction and fact."* No sooner did the future Nobel physicist realize this than he dropped out of Sunday school in disdain and never went back. A bar mitzvah was de rigueur for a Jewish Far Rockaway boy, but this one balked at learning a Hebrew passage to chant in the temple just for a wingding in his honor afterward and a pile of presents. His atheist father, possibly admiring his son's precocious unbelief, let the custom slide. So Richard Feynman may never in all his life have looked into a Torah scroll; too bad if so, for these scrolls are a remarkable try at INVARIANCE, a holy grail of theoretical physics.

Invariance? Why, yes. In the art of writing, so far as human will and skill can achieve it, invariance.

The Jewish faith, old style, today has two alternate denominations, some minor departures, and some fringe

---

* *James Gleick,* Genius: The Life and Science of Richard Feynman *(New York: Vintage, 1993).*

sects. Invariant in all, sacred to all, present in all is a *Sefer Torah,* a "Book of the Law," wrapped in a mantle and kept in a Holy Ark, so called be it a plain wooden cupboard for one scroll, or an ornate two-story marble sanctum for the banked-up scrolls of a wealthy congregation. A Sefer Torah is the Five Books of Moses handwritten in black ink on one long roll of animal skin, as copied and recopied by many generations of scribes for well over two thousand years. The presence of a Sefer Torah alone—nothing else—makes a hotel room, or a hired auditorium, or a local theater, or the social hall of a friendly church (on which usage some frown), or a neighborhood synagogue, or a grandiose metropolitan temple, or the small converted private house where I pray daily, a House of God. The scroll must be accurate to the letter, scanned today by computer. Exhaustive Talmudic rules grip the writing of a scroll in iron tradition.

In the days when my family summered on Fire Island we would hold Sabbath services in our home, with a scroll written for me long ago by a Jerusalem scribe at my grandfather's behest. One morning the rabbi chanting the Torah section thought he spotted a flaw in one letter. On the instant the scroll became unusable, and next day a graybeard scribe of high repute traveled from Brooklyn by subway, commuter train, and ferry to have a look at the letter. It was questionable, he fixed it with his quill pen and mandated ink, and went back to Brooklyn, fee and expenses paid, sacredness of my scroll restored. A droll anecdote, you may say, but everyone knows that copyist errors and variant readings in old texts are as inevitable as the rusting of iron or the weathering of stone. Modern Bible critics smile at this presumption of invariance in a text handed down by Ezra the Scribe—so tradition holds—six centuries before the time of Yeshu of Nazareth, who quoted the Torah often in his sermons and parables, and said of its invariance, *"Heaven and earth will pass away, but not one jot or tittle of the Law will fail."*

In 1947, an obscure development of Bible archeology spiked in the media and reverberated out to the general public. Bedouin goatherds came upon jars containing pre-Christian copies of the Hebrew Bible in desolate caves by the Dead Sea. These were mostly fragments, but the Book of Isaiah was complete, and scholars found that it fairly agreed with the text in our *Tanakh,* the Hebrew Bible; and a fragment from the Book of Leviticus quite paralleled the passage as penned by the Jerusalem scribe in my scroll, now used in the Palm Springs synagogue. Invariance, no, not quite; amazement, well, yes; shake-up of settled academic views, yes, indeed.

Years ago I viewed the Dead Sea Scrolls in an underground wing of Jerusalem's Israel Museum, the Shrine of the Book, which has a picturesque rooftop like the lid of a

Dead Sea cave jar. Biblical Jerusalem is a sort of religious Disneyland for tourists on the run, and the shrine is one of its prime rides into the past of the Jewish people and of Christian belief; but of course Disneyland is all entertaining fakery, and biblical Jerusalem is as real as the Holy Land earth under the pavement, an exalting jolt of authenticity for even the farthest drifted Jew. A New York woman of fashion I knew well, the wife of my publisher, spent a day whizzing around Jerusalem's biblical sights, then wrote me a thrilled letter, concluding, "Now I can't *wait* to read the Old Testament."

The scrolls were on exhibit in San Diego for a while, so I saw again those skins darkened by time to deep brown, marked in a strange Paleo-Hebrew alphabet readable only by scholarly specialists. The soaring, thundering music of Isaiah is there in those dim hen tracks, a voice sounding across three millennia, quoted in granite outside the United Nations building in New York: *"They shall beat their swords into plowshares, and their spears into pruning hooks. Nation shall not lift sword against nation, neither shall they learn war any more."* That inscription will weather away, may become indecipherable, or the building itself may not last that long. No matter, the voice of Isaiah will be heard, it now seems clear, in the language of man while the art of writing lasts. At the closest human approach, that is invariance.

L'Envoi

My effort to picture Richard Feynman's Big Stage and New Drama stops here, where written history begins. The rest is in books and documents beyond counting. The Core Curriculum offered to me and my nephew, and offers today, a digest of the New Drama complete to modern times. My nephew challenged me to make it fit with the far terser Old Drama, which starts, *"In the beginning God created the heavens and the earth."*

Here goes.

CHAPTER SIX

Leyte/Auschwitz

S. Y. Agnon once remarked to me in his Jerusalem home, with a wave of a warning finger, *"Remember, Herman Wouk, we are storytellers. Stories, pictures, people! No thoughts."* Wise old Agnon, Nobelist in literature, wickedly witty little skull-capped genius, bless his memory! He pointed the way for me to meet the challenge; too much thought already in these pages. Neither a theologian nor a scientist, I tell stories. In telling the story that first led me to seek out Feynman, I gradually integrated the New Drama and the Old in my mind and spirit, as well as I ever will; not through reasoning about faith and science but by creating pictures.

First Picture: Gog and Magog

The picture I started with, the scarcely remembered Battle of Leyte Gulf, was far, far removed from what became my abiding theme.

The armadas that clashed at Leyte Gulf are as outmoded today as Hannibal's elephants; with some rue I say that, for in October 1944, when Admiral Halsey's immense task groups sortied from Ulithi atoll, I was there. My ship towed targets for their gunnery practice. The battle was fought over five days and millions of square miles of ocean, the largest fleet action of all time. The upshot was that Halsey steamed his grandiose array of battleships and aircraft carriers two hundred miles north and two hundred miles south *and never fired his guns except in target practice;* the botched victory was won by valiant minor forces and a lot of luck. Opposing the American attempt to retake the Philippines, the entire surviving Japanese navy under Admiral Kurita sailed out to crush the invasion at all cost. Kurita fought his way through to Leyte Gulf with heavy losses and had the landing forces under his guns, whereupon, *without firing a shot at them, he turned away and fled back to Japan.**

This blind blundering of two befuddled old men, entrusted with gargantuan armed forces and the fate of nations, struck me as the germ of a big novel about modern war. For the fictional element, I envisioned interlocking the families of principal characters serving at Leyte Gulf, so that their crisscrossing stories would cover all the war theaters. I even bethought me of a suitably portentous biblical title: *Gog and Magog.* Such a project meant much research

---

* *A scherzo sketch, not inaccurate, of a mighty sea fight that spans 64 pages in my* War and Remembrance.

far afield from Leyte Gulf, of course, though the first book I read was *Admiral Halsey's Story,* rushed out pell-mell after the war in a magazine serial and then in hardcover, in which he carefully explained that he had made no mistakes at Leyte Gulf. Over the years, as I accumulated and read books and made notes, the Leyte Gulf book came to be called in my diary "the main task." *The Caine Mutiny* gave my name a sound, the publication of *Marjorie Morningstar* brought an avalanche of Jewish distractions, and I retreated to the Virgin Islands; where I wrote *Youngblood Hawke,* a trial run for the main task in length, complexity, and distance from my own background.

There are no Jews in *Youngblood Hawke.* The novel is a magic carpet ride through the Arabian Nights of a bestselling author's life—women, Hollywood, money, taxes, celebrity, much of it quite funny—with somber subplots of a Kentucky coal lawsuit, a congressional investigation, and a real-estate bankruptcy. Hawke comes to New York from a Kentucky mining town with an untidy manuscript in a satchel. His raw narrative gift sets off a devil dance of commercial exploitation and attracts the wrong women. His flying carpet crashes and kills him early. Jewish characters are there, all right, recognizable enough under their assimilated names—Prince, Tulking, Givney, Winter, and so on, their roots shrugged off, easy targets for satire—and satiric American Jewish novels and authors were then much in vogue, but I forbore. The shrouded fate of the European Jews was haunting me.

Allied armies had uncovered the massacre, but in its full enormity it was still undocumented and ungrasped. The Eichmann trial lay years in the future, the term *Holocaust* was not yet common coin, and little though I really knew about it, the horror shadowed my earlier writings. The lawyer Barney Greenwald, rebuking the *Caine* officers after the court martial, speaks of corpses cooked down to soap, an old British atrocity ploy in which he naively believes; Marjorie's last romantic involvement, before she settles down in suburbia, is with a stranger she meets on the *Queen Mary,* a bleak man of mystery who rescues Jews from the Nazis. Yet for the life of me I could not see how the fate of European Jewry, though foursquare in the time frame of Leyte Gulf, could be part of my story. This troubled me more and more as I worked and read on.

Second Picture: Raul Hilberg

On our breezy patio in Saint Thomas overlooking the Caribbean and the Atlantic, I was writing away at *Youngblood Hawke* when my wife brought me a magazine. "You're going to write about Europe," she said, though I had never told her that. "Better read this." It was a dazzling review by the British historian H. R. Trevor-Roper, renowned author of *The Last Days of Hitler,* of a book called *The Destruction of the European Jews.* Such informed praise compelled attention. I ordered the book, a thick brown volume printed in hard-to-read double columns. No matter, once I started it I drove straight through and wrote the author, one Raul Hilberg at the University of Vermont, asking to meet him.

Hilberg seemed surprised at my visit and ill at ease. He laid on sherry and cookies in his modest digs, for academics and their spouses eager to meet a popular novelist. When I mentioned why I was there, the blank looks and vague comments betrayed that none of them had read Hilberg's book or even the Trevor-Roper review. The young associate professor had gotten something published on a remote repulsive subject, so what? Among them he had not grown one academic inch. Nor did that appear to trouble Hilberg, though he was hard to figure out. Next day we went for a walk, and as I had done years before with I. Bernard Cohen, I uncorked a long harangue—my vision of a big war book centered on the Battle of Leyte Gulf, my awareness that the massacre had been going on at the same time, my inability to connect the two events, since they had happened in two different wars on opposite sides of the globe; and my conviction nevertheless, after reading his book, that I had to link the battle and the Jewish fate or drop the project.

We ambled a considerable way through pleasant university grounds as I put my dilemma to him. Hilberg walked on for a while in silence then said, "You've got to go to

Germany." Those were his first words. My reply, vehement and immediate, was that I had resolved never to set foot on that cursed soil. "Yes, yes, I know. You've got to go to Germany." He left it at that to speak about his own work, and a fierce wounded pride glowed through his dour demeanor. His book had started as a PhD thesis at Columbia. His mentor had warned him that the obnoxious subject would not help and could well mar his academic career; but if he persisted, he had to find a structure to sustain the huge undertaking. And in fact, after toiling through mountains of documents, he had found his structure in a decision to make the thesis a study not of the victims but of the perpetrators. "You have to find your structure," he kept saying, as we walked and talked for hours. That was what I took away with me; that, and the imperative to go to Germany.

So I did go to the "cursed soil." A durable bestseller there was *Die Caine war ihr Schicksal ("The Caine Was His Destiny")*, and I found I could talk to anybody, up to and including the prime minister. I met a wide range of Germans, even lectured at a university, and soon absorbed Hilberg's point. Germany was not a nightmare land of heel-clicking movie sadists and comedy boobs, but a lovely old-world country much like France and England, with people not too different from ourselves. This brought the Hitler era nearer reality, made the Holocaust even more mystifying and horrible, and enabled me to write about the Germans.

Raul Hilberg was a bitter atheist, and I have known no man more entitled to that view. Down the years when we met we never talked religion, though a daughter of his went to Israel and turned orthodox. He lived out his academic career at the University of Vermont, and I was among the speakers at his retirement banquet. Holocaust scholars, filmmakers, political scientists, and journalists came from all over to do him honor. The event was a disorderly crowded mess. The university hosts were overwhelmed, unaware to the last, it seemed, that the author of a mighty twentieth-century masterwork had been among them.

Third Picture: Admiral Gallery

Flashback to March 1951. *The Caine Mutiny* came out to a quiet slow start except in the U.S. Navy, where straightaway it raised a noise. No such captain as Queeg ever existed! Pure tripe, tommyrot, libel on the service, etc., etc.! A letter arrived with the flags of a rear admiral on the return address, and I braced for a hammering. "Best book about the modern navy that I've ever read," the admiral wrote, and asked to meet me. In the Oak Room bar at the Plaza, a short man in a brown suit and red bow tie, with a lean weathered face, approached and held out a hand. "Herman Wouk? Dan Gallery." Pleasantries over, the admiral disclosed that—like me when I asked to meet

Hilberg—he wanted something. In his rare spare time he had begun selling articles and short stories to magazines, and he needed an agent. At my behest, my own top-level agent took him on.

"Cast your bread upon the waters," says Ecclesiastes in the Old Drama, *"after many days you will find it."* Not long after that rendezvous, Gallery invited me on a training cruise of his carrier group. He ensconced me in his flag cabin and ordered his chief steward to figure out what I could eat by my rules. At his elbow on the flying bridge day and night, I observed spectacular landings and takeoffs; also dangled on a helicopter cable to visit a submarine, and returning to port, got catapulted off the ship in a fighter plane. As a retired reserve lieutenant, I could risk my naval neck as the admiral pleased. The picture of Victor Henry in my novels owes much to those days at sea, watching Dan Gallery in his mode of hard-edged command.

This brainy maverick sea dog, a practicing Catholic, and I, a maverick Jewish novelist who keeps kosher, formed a bizarre long-lasting friendship. By the time he retired from the Navy to a Virginia suburb and was churning out salable novels, humorous short stories, and salty lucubrations on public affairs, I was back in the States and settled in Washington, D.C. for the research resources there, to get at *Gog and Magog* in earnest. The richest resource turned out to be Admiral Gallery. He opened all Navy doors for me. I had access to confidences, on the highest level, about the major sea battles—Midway, Leyte Gulf, the submarine campaign—and the men in command. A unifying structure still eluded me, but nearing fifty and desperate, I took the plunge and wrote a laborious false start. Then I wrote another. On a third try I cobbled up a chapter or so about a senior Navy officer and his family, which seemed sort of alive. How to link him to the Holocaust, how even to get him to Leyte Gulf? All was dark, black dark. Gallery had been sending me his book drafts right along for comment. Now turnabout, I sent him the chapter, and he came into town to talk about it. When he said, "Why not send Victor Henry to Germany as naval attaché?" a star shell soared up in the dark, and—only because Raul Hilberg had sent me there years earlier—I caught a glimmer of the long-sought structure: the way to connect Victor Henry to the other principal figure I had borne in mind for years and years, in whose life and death the Old and the New Dramas would merge.

Who was this figure?

Fourth Picture: Aaron Jastrow

As Rome was falling to the Allies in June 1944, an advance patrol of GIs found the elderly philosopher George Santayana, Irwin Edman's idol, at work on his memoirs in an apartment of a convent while artillery still thumped outside. Asked how he could stand living in a Fascist country at war with America, Santayana placidly rejoined, "There are good and bad in all systems." Much as I admired Santayana, when I read about this, perhaps in a tattered *Time* magazine at sea, it irritated me. In my early notes for the big war book, I merged Santayana with Bernard Berenson, the eminent Jewish art connoisseur who spent the war unscathed in his posh villa outside Florence, in the figure of a complacent Yale historian retired to a villa near Sienna on the proceeds of a bestseller. He would be an agnostic humanist like Berenson; but unlike him, not protected by his wealth and connections, he would fall into Nazi claws.

In time Edman blended into this phantom, as did Harry Wolfson, a major Harvard scholar of religion at home in the Talmud. All four were bachelors. Berenson and Wolfson had both come from Lithuania as children, acquiring U.S. citizenship through their immigrant fathers; and I foresaw this technicality as the trip wire of the historian's doom. A fifth person was always part of the amalgam, though shadowy, indefinable, something like a disembodied voice. Once an astute friend of Gallery's, Admiral Eli Reich, was reviewing with me the submarine scenes in my typescript of *War and Remembrance*. Cocking his head and looking me in the eye, he said, "Herman, you're Aaron Jastrow, aren't you?" Eli Reich was the only American submarine captain who ever sank a battleship.* I didn't argue with him.

---

* Kongo, *damaged at Leyte Gulf; sunk a month later by* Sealion, *Eli Reich commanding.*

Actually, I had come upon a conceivable tie between Henry and Jastrow sometime before I sent my chapter to old Dan. A Trollope novel I was reading, *Nina Balatka,* began with these words: "Nina Balatka was a maiden of Prague, born of Christian parents, and herself a Christian—but she loved a Jew, and this is her story." *Aha!* (Novelists have those, as well as scientists.) Reverse the religions, Navy man's Christian son loves professor's Jewish niece; *that* was the tie that had glimmered under Gallery's star shell. Now, with Pug Henry in Germany and Jastrow and his niece, Natalie, in Italy, instinct growled, *"This thing can work, let's go already."* The romance sprang to life, the main task took off, and characters came thronging into existence around Henry, Jastrow, and the young lovers, from the South Pacific to the Soviet Union, in both directions around the globe.

Fifth Picture: Armin von Roon

A relatively merry run of piled-up pages ensued for about a year, then slowed and stopped. I had made one simple, fundamental, fatal mistake. Crisscrossing the stories of characters in different war theaters did not convey the war picture. Their experiences were fragmentary. Their awareness was limited. Only at the exalted level of Hitler, Stalin, Roosevelt, Churchill, and their cadres of advisers, was the whole global conflict in sight through the fog of war. My people could know only the living moment around them, plus the little they read or heard. My belief in the book quaked. Sags of spirit are a writer's lot, but this halt was new. It was a collapse.

Remodeling had driven me out of our house just then. I was working at the Cosmos Club in a small sunless bedroom, staring stumped at a blank yellow legal pad, when there walked into the book a new figure unplanned, unrelated to anyone in the plot, nameless and wholly alien to me. Walked into the book, I say, and launched on a précis of the war's outbreak and the Polish campaign, all England's fault. When at rare times the words come pouring out like that, I let them pour. Blue pencils are cheap. That evening I brought home a sheaf of yellow pages scrawled in a few feverish hours, and after dinner I read them aloud as usual to my wife, amidst the doleful wreckage of our living room. She broke in almost at once. "What on earth are you doing? You *can't* stop the story dead for that stuff. Anyway, the fellow doesn't sound German, he writes too well and clearly."

"He's studied Churchill and de Gaulle on World War One. He's a brain, he's picked up style. Anyway, I do this or quit."

A skeptical look, a shrug. "Oh, don't quit." She was right, of course, but I was right, too. The interloper was a mere brainstorm, yet when instinct trumps craft in the novel art, it can prove a lucky leap forward. The poltergeist acquired body, name, and life as a Prussian officer, General Armin von Roon, serving twenty years in Spandau for war crimes, and spending his prison years writing an exhaustive military history, *Land, Sea, and Air Operations of World War II,* each operation prefaced by a clear strategic summary. After his death these brief summaries would be compiled and published in Germany as a popular history of the war, and Pug Henry in retirement would translate the book, now and then correcting Roon's German myopia with interposed comments, tart Dan Gallery style.

This odd stereoscopic structure held up. A cyclorama of the whole war gradually took shape, campaign by campaign, battle by battle, summit by summit, seen from the other side of the hill. Against this backdrop my people played out their lives, sometimes in settings half a world apart. Thus when Vice Admiral Victor Henry, commanding a division of new battleships, steams north and then south under Halsey, his giant gun turrets maddeningly silent, Aaron Jastrow and his niece are being summoned to board the train to Auschwitz, and the simultaneity is a fact. The last transport to Auschwitz left the "Paradise Ghetto" outside Prague as the Battle of Leyte Gulf was ending; and the long-sought link of the battle to the destruction of the European Jews turned out to be the death in a gas chamber of Aaron Jastrow, for whom in his last days on earth, the Old and New Dramas became one.

Sixth Picture: Berel Jastrow

A noted nuclear physicist asked me, when I gave a talk at Caltech, "How could you keep telling one story for fourteen years? Didn't you get bored with the characters?" Two motives kept me going, I replied: grief over the catastrophe to the Jews, and pride in America's resurgence from the Pearl Harbor debacle to world leadership. A third strong motive I discern only now, thinking back over decades to the time I was writing the books; *zest,* sheer zest for a new challenge in my fifties, to bring history to life with a storyteller's art. Hence, Armin von Roon; hence, travels with my wife to Leningrad, Stalingrad, Moscow, Tehran, where the plot takes Pug Henry; hence, our long scenic journey from Siena via Elba and Corsica to Marseilles, to track the route of Jastrow and his niece fleeing a Javert of the SS. And hence, our hard days in Auschwitz.

The core of the main task became the story of Victor Henry and his two Navy sons, a submariner and a fighter pilot, and their women; the Jastrow tale wove through it in the romance and wartime marriage of the submariner and the niece. Armin von Roon bridges both narratives, and impatient readers of the novels may skip him now and then to find out what happens next. Not a federal offense. A historian of note told me, with a sort of guilty grin, that he skimmed the story parts to read Armin von Roon. Far from vexing me, he made my day, for who or what is

"Armin von Roon" after all but a puppet, voicing in fictive fashion my decades of delving?

That research, however, went much beyond the ken of a Prussian general. Writing scenes set in Auschwitz—the gigantic slave labor area and death camp as it was day by day, crematorium smoke, smell and all, not the manicured tourist museum we visited—cried for a major Auschwitz presence. Aaron's younger cousin, Berel Jastrow, became that presence. Berel shows up briefly in *The Winds of War.* In *War and Remembrance* he comes into his own. The cousins, childhood chums in the yeshiva, grow up poles apart: Aaron the agnostic Yale historian, his Talmud learning dropped as a boyish game; Berel the prosperous Warsaw merchant, diligent Talmudist and Old Drama believer.

Berel Jastrow was Raul Hilberg's favorite character; strange that an irreconcilable atheist should so admire a devout Jew, but there you are. "A haunting surreal presence," Raul called him, and indeed Berel's adventures, strictly grounded though they are in survivor documentation, take on a mystic aura. He seems to bear a charm. While Aaron sinks into the Nazi quicksand with his niece and her baby son, Louis, groping to fathom what is happening to them, Berel escapes from Auschwitz and traverses the Polish back country, through many a hairbreadth exploit and Dickensian coincidence, to cross the Czech border and bring rolls of death-camp films to the Allies via the Prague resistance. Not the least of the coincidences is the way he finds out that Aaron, whom he has not seen in fifty years, is alive nearby. The partisan in Prague to whom he delivers the films, a nondescript dentist, remarks on his odd name, "There's a Jastrow here in Theresienstadt, some damn fool American author who got caught traveling illegally in France."

"*Aaron* Jastrow?" says Berel.

CHAPTER SEVEN

Aaron/Berel

Seventh Picture: Awakening of a Humanist

World War II, "my war," has receded into the history books, the master theses, and the old action movies on late-night TV; and the bizarre Theresienstadt hoax has dimmed from sight, but the visit of the Danish Red Cross to the old army town—the only inside look ever allowed to neutrals—happened as my novel tells it. So did the "Great Beautification,"* the frantic cover-up beforehand ordered by Adolf Eichmann. Aaron Jastrow is shaken out of his humanist slumbers to serve in Eichmann's cover-up, and his ordeal is fiction, of course, but the ghetto narrative is fact. In "The Paradise Ghetto," part 6 of *War and Remembrance,* the main war chronicle runs with Armin von Roon and the Henry story from the Russian breakthrough at

---

* *Grosse Verschönerungsaktion.*

Kursk to the start of Leyte Gulf, while a few sparse scenes in Theresienstadt speed Aaron Jastrow to his doom.

This town reserved for privileged Jews—distinguished musicians, artists, judges, decorated Jewish war veterans, and the like—was reported by the German-controlled European press as such an idyllic and luxurious resort, with staged photographs and faked interviews, that deluded rich Jews paid the Gestapo huge sums in advance for leases on nonexistent apartments there. The reality was a barracks town for five thousand troops jammed with forty thousand Jews or more, who on arrival were all stripped of possessions and turned loose to live in squalor, disease, and hunger, until transports took off thousands at a swoop for "resettlement in the east." Nobody knew exactly what "the east" meant, and few wanted to believe or talk about the ghastly rumors.

Theresienstadt was in fact a sluice to Auschwitz, nothing more, for these privileged Jews; but while the reprieve lasted they danced at cafés where there was no food or drink, organized quartets, concerts, lectures, even an operetta, and produced remarkable art works now prized by collectors, while hearses rolled by daily with piled-up dead. Some of the art is on view today in a "Terezín Memorial Museum," a forlorn Holocaust sideshow in that out-of-the-way Czech town. Aaron Jastrow's diary, *A Jew's Journey*, recounts much of this. When he and his niece are trapped by Italy's joining the war, he begins it in a Santayana echo of ironic detachment, as a sort of follow-up to his bestseller, *A Jew's Jesus,* but by the time he and Natalie chute into Theresienstadt, the writing has turned dark, terse, and grim. Here is how the entry about his encounter with Eichmann begins.

> It will not be easy to record my meeting with Obersturmbannführer Adolf Eichmann. In a sense I am starting this narrative over; and not only this narrative! Whatever I have written, all my life long, now seems to have been composed in a child's dream.
>
> What I must put down is so dangerous that the former hiding place of my papers will not do.... I have discovered a more secure place. Not even Natalie will know about it.... If I survive the war, I will find these papers where I hid them.

At sixty-five Aaron Jastrow has yet to endure real maltreatment. As a yeshiva boy he once dared to ask whether the demons described in the Talmud actually existed, and Reb Laizar's reply was a stinging slap and, "Out, *shaygetz* [heathen], out!" It has long been his jest that Reb Laizar's slap sparked his apostasy, for he took refuge from the snowstorm outside in a church. In Theresienstadt violent abuse is commonplace: an old woman clubbed to the ground for peddling forbidden cigarette butts, an SS man laying a Jew's head bloodily open for failing to give his name as required, "I am the stinking Jew, Mandelbaum." But these things have been happening to other people. Aaron has kept his head down, his *"I am the stinking Jew, Jastrow"* loud, prompt, and clear, and as librarian of the rich and growing collection of looted Judaica, he has thus far stayed out of trouble. He has even risked teaching a few boys Talmud in the library, to pass the time and bask in their admiration.

Now the commandant summons him to his office to meet Adolf Eichmann, only a name to Jastrow but a fearsome one. He obeys with trepidation and is pleasantly surprised. He writes: *"Except for the intimidating black uniforms of Eichmann and the commandant, I might have been calling on a bank manager to discuss a loan."* The summons is to appoint him as Elder for Cultural Affairs, a new department in the sham governing council of Jews. These Elders are regarded as cringing sellouts. They manage garbage collection and such municipal services, enforce SS rules and orders, and lie to the press about the happy state of the lucky Theresienstadt Jews. Jastrow humbly tries to decline the honor, whereupon Eichmann's brisk cordial manner dissolves in a Jekyll/Hyde change. He crazily screeches through a twisted mouth, *"Who do you think you are? Where the devil do you think you are?"* The commandant springs at Jastrow, knocks him off his chair, and kicks him around as he lies on the floor, kicks and kicks him, bellowing obscene threats, until a hard kick aimed directly at the base of Jastrow's spine sends electric pain shooting through him. At the desk Eichmann smokes a cigarette, quite Dr. Jekyll again. The commandant forces Jastrow to get up on his knees and shout, over and over, *"I'm an old bag of filthy Jewish shit."* That is that.

He is brought to a council chamber to be photographed with the Elders. A pretty young German reporter chats with the Elder for Culture, Dr. Aaron Jastrow, well-known American author of *A Jew's Jesus,* taking notes, and Jastrow realizes that Natalie and he are now beyond diplomatic rescue. The gloss he lends to the hoax outweighs any trouble the State Department might give the Germans about him. In the diary, Jastrow concludes his detailed account of the whole episode so:

> What I did when I returned to my room will perhaps make sense to nobody but me. For the first time in about fifty years I put on phylacteries. I borrowed them from a pious old man next door. The worn black-stained leather boxes gave me no instant intellectual or spiritual uplift, of course, as I strapped them on head and arm, yet I will persist in this while I live. Thus I answer Eichmann. Reb Laizar slapped me out of my Jewish identity, as it were, and an SS officer kicked me back into it.

Is this a return to the old Jewish God? Never mind. He and I both have accounts to settle, for if I have to explain my apostasy, He has to explain Theresienstadt and worse, if the rumors about the transports are true, as I now believe they are. My lifelong posture of learned agnostic humanism was all very fine. My books about Christianity are not without merit. But taking it all in all, I have spent my life on the run. Now I turn and stand. I am a Jew.

Eighth Picture: Udam

A new commandant of evil repute, SS Sturmbannführer Rahm, summons the Council of Elders and issues astonishing orders. *"No more idiotic saluting and removing of caps! No more 'stinking Jew' talk! No more of all that shit! Theresienstadt is not a concentration camp, it is a comfortable and happy residential town!"* The ghetto is to be smartened up forthwith: a beautiful park, a spacious children's playground, spic-and-span hospitals and schoolrooms, a renovated community center with studios, lecture halls, a theater, and an opera house; cabarets to be redecorated, more orchestras and an opera company to be created, all manner of entertainments devised and rehearsed. Rahm walks out, leaving the stunned Elders looking at each other. Eppstein, the *Ältester* (High Elder), a meek beaten-down sociologist who serves as mayor, rises to announce that there is one more thing. The new commandant finds the overcrowding most unhealthy and unsightly, so five thousand Jews must be transported at once.

A pall falls on the ghetto. Aaron Jastrow is terrified, not for himself but for Natalie. Ignoring his warnings, she has been doing puppet shows that lampoon the Germans, with a nervy ghetto denizen called Udam. This cantor's son performs regularly in the SS cafés outside the walls, war ballads like "Lili Marlene" that make them weep in their beer, or salacious songs that set them roaring, the dirtier the better, or he can even do a cantorial passage as a Yid novelty. So Udam may be safe, but Natalie has put her little boy and herself in peril. Since he became an Elder, Aaron can do nothing with her. Obviously she thinks her selfish old uncle jumped at the despicable role just to save his own hide. She does as she pleases.

When she meets Udam to rehearse the puppet show that will follow the evening lecture, he shows her the gray transport card he has received. She panics at the sight, but he reassures her that she's all right; she and her uncle have the highest exemption. As for himself, he has pulled all the Jewish strings, has even talked to the SS. Nothing doing, he goes. Nevertheless he will not hear of calling off this last show. Why? With his new jokes for the puppets he actually makes her laugh. It will be their best show ever!

A workshop note.

In 1977 my astute editor, Larned Bradford, flew out to my Palm Springs lair to read War and Remembrance *in draft typescript. He said when he finished it, "Herman, this book was a religious obligation, wasn't it?* The Winds of War *was just a warm-up." Dead on! Ever since "the big war book" split in two,* Winds *in my mind had been the pedestal,* Remembrance *the memorial. Old Ned did not have to mention the scene that prompted his comment, any more than Eli Reich did when he asked, "Herman, you're Aaron Jastrow, aren't you?" I wrote that scene one afternoon in Bermuda, when my wife and I were supposedly on vacation. It came to me, so I banged it out on my portable, and read it to her in some excitement. "It's a good sermon," the love of my life said. Nothing more. Next to her, the Sphinx was a talking head. Again, dead on! Of course I am not Aaron Jastrow, but that is the nearest I have come, or am ever likely to come, to setting down in words what I believe. The sermon in full, "Heroes of the* Iliad," *closes this little book as a sort of coda.*

Ninth Picture: The Scene of the Sermon

In the packed audience for the lecture there is no lively chatter, rather a funereal silence. The puppet theater is folded to a side. The Elder for Culture mounts a crude lectern, notes in hand, and in pedantic German starts by contrasting *Troilus and Cressida,* Shakespeare's play about the heroes of the *Iliad,* with Homer's far more profound portrayals. He then compares the implied Greek religious outlook—quarrelsome gods, a purposeless universe, "atoms moving in a void"—to the Jewish idea of one just Creator and his Law for mankind. So far Natalie thinks, this is just Hebraism and Hellenism again, the theme of *A Jew's Jesus,* but it takes a turn that confounds her.

Stepping down from the lectern without his notes, her uncle stands there, his lips working, then he bursts out to measure the *Iliad* against the Book of Job *in Yiddish!* "My dear Jewish friends, the Talmud tells us," he begins, "that Job was never born and never existed, he was a parable." Gone, any echo of Santayana's irony about religion; Aaron Jastrow is sounding like a *maggid,* a popular preacher of the shtetls, as he goes on to personify in the audience before him, many of whom have gray cards, the suffering Job. His hearers come alive, faces alight, hungry for his words. This outpouring in *mama lashon,* mother language, rises in wave upon passionate wave of Yiddish, to a bitter acceptance of senseless disaster, and of faith, faith however tortured, faith in Job's incomprehensible living Redeemer.... Aaron breaks off, stares in long silence at the audience, stumbles to his seat. Udam gestures to Natalie *"no puppets,"* gets to his feet and begins chanting the Yom Kippur cantorial that has earned him his ghetto name.

Udam—Udam—Udam

(*Udam* is Polish Yiddish for *Adam,* "Man." The audience at once responds in a low chorus: *"Udam...Udam... Udam...")*

Man—Man—Man
Man is of the dust and returns to dust
Udam...Udam...Udam...
He is like the clay jug that breaks, the flower that fades...
Udam...Udam...Udam...
The passing cloud, the dream that flies away...
Udam...Udam...Udam...

Udam begins to dance like an old rabbi, takes Aaron's hand, and together they step round and round, hands upraised as in prayer; then Udam shifts to a lively old song of messianic hope, and as they dance faster, the audience rises to clap in rhythm:

Oy let the Temple be rebuilt
Oy speedily in our time
Oy and grant us a portion in Your Law!

Outside the barracks the audience disperses, stirred and consoled. A tall figure in a shabby yellow-starred jacket sidles up to Aaron and mutters in Yiddish, *"Gut gezugt, Arele, und gut getantzed."* ("Well said, little Aaron, and well danced.") Aaron peers at a burly old man with bushy gray hair and a clean-shaven face; a stranger, yet there is something in the voice, in the smile...

"Berel?"

Tenth Picture: The Last Train to Auschwitz

Late October 1944. The ghetto is dying. The Red Cross visit has long since come and gone. The cover-up worked. The Danes were satisfied, or at least reported that they were. A few old Jews creep around the abandoned garbage-strewn streets of Eichmann's Potemkin village, pilfering firewood from the decaying facades. Like all the remaining *Prominente,* the Elder of Culture and his niece have their gray cards. The advancing Red Army has overrun one death camp in Poland—the Germans scoff at this as a Soviet fabrication—and the Allies are closing in from the west. The

SS is in great haste to get their job done. This last transport will be jammed.

Even now the Jews do not know their destination, and the will not to believe still prevails. Berel told Aaron the entire ghastly truth. Natalie does not know all and hardly cares, treasuring more than life a photograph smuggled to her weeks ago: her little boy, Louis, chubby and smiling, standing with Berel near a haystack! On the lecture night, Berel proposed a wildly risky scheme to get Louis, whom he called *der osed,* the future, out of the ghetto. She refused, then gave in when Rahm threatened a horrible death for Louis if she at all bungled her role in hoaxing the Danes. Once the child was gone she agonized through months of uncertainty and regret, until one night a shadowy woman in passing slipped the picture into her hand. Now she has it, her son, *"the future,"* is all right, let come what may.

Chapter 92 of War and Remembrance *is Armin von Roon's biting analysis of the Battle of Leyte Gulf, summing up, "the Americans stumbled, fumbled, and flopped into a sorry 'victory.'" Pug Henry's sharp professional rejoinder, granting Halsey's blunders, portrays the victory as hard-fought and honorable.*

Chapter 93 depicts the last train to Auschwitz, from the loading of the Jews in Theresienstadt, to their arrival at the ramp in Birkenau. Natalie is selected for slave labor. Aaron and all the *Prominente* go with the women and children to the gas. Natalie's three-day ordeal of hunger and choking thirst in the cattle car, amid suffering, sickness, and death all around her, owes much to my research in survivor accounts. Aaron's death is all imaginary. Nobody ever survived gassing to write about it.

The story follows him down into the bunker, into the undressing room, into the gas chamber, to his very last moments, gasping *"Hear O Israel, the Lord our God is One God,"* as the life is crushed out of him by naked bodies falling and piling on top of him. It follows his dead body into the crematorium oven, and it follows his ashes next day as they float down the Vistula through his native Poland to the Baltic Sea.

Chapter 94 of the novel depicts Byron Henry, newly in command of a submarine and forced to the surface by depth charges, winning a running battle with a Japanese destroyer.

These jarring juxtapositions are of course at the heart of the "structure" that I owe to Raul Hilberg. An able, if owlish, European historian asked me, after vetting *War and Remembrance* in typescript, "Why didn't you write two books, one about the war, one about the Holocaust?" Owls do not see well by daylight.

From the next to last page of *War and Remembrance:*

> In a shallow, hastily dug grave in the wood outside Prague, Berel Jastrow's bones lie unmarked, like so many bones all over Europe. And so this story ends.
>
> It is only a story, of course. Berel Jastrow was never born and never existed. He was a parable. In truth his bones stretch from the French coast to the Urals, dry bones of a murdered giant. And in truth a marvelous thing happens; his story does not end there, for the bones stand up and take on flesh. God breathes spirit into the bones, and Berel Jastrow turns eastward and goes home.

Aaron Jastrow was never born and never existed. Santayana, Berenson, Wolfson were real people, as am I. Characters in fiction are composites or inventions. Fiction entertains; parable endures. Can Aaron be called a parable? Can Berel? If my work lasts down the years, readers will know.

CHAPTER EIGHT

Last Picture: The Fourth Conversation

After our three conversations in Aspen, Richard Feynman and I never met again. Call this chapter my last pass at parable.

A Walk in Georgetown

Sunk in a soft lobby armchair of the Cosmos Club, I watch the door for a friend late for lunch. In walks a gaunt man with a long mane of gray hair and a careworn look. He drops in a deep armchair near me, picks up the *Washington Post* from a side table, glances at me in surprise.

"You're Wouk. "

Adopting his brusque note, "You're Feynman."

"You're the Talmud guy in Aspen. You write novels."

"I write novels, and yes, study Talmud a bit."

"You sent me a book of yours. I didn't read it."

"Well, fiction can't interest you compared to the marvels of nature you work on. So you told me in Aspen."

Enigmatic grin I first saw at Caltech so long ago. A shade rueful now. "I suppose I could have said that."

Someone he knows comes in and waves. He gets himself out of the armchair, saying, "What are you doing after lunch?"

"Walking back to my house in Georgetown."

"I'm due at Georgetown University around three. Let's walk together."

"Sure."

Outside the club, a fine April day. We walk down Florida Avenue, across the P Street bridge, and take my shortcut to N Street, a leafy dirt path along the ridge above Rock Creek Parkway. In Aspen he did most of the talking with cheerful ebullience. Today he is quiet. The silence grows long, but this walk was his idea.

"Why do you live in this godforsaken town?" he says at last. "You could live anywhere."

"I came here to do research." He gives me a puzzled side-glance. "For that *War and Peace* of World War Two, if you remember."

"Oh, that, yes."

"My wife and I got to like it here, so we stayed."

"They told me at lunch you wrote two enormous books along that line."

"It came out that way."

Dirt crunching underfoot for a while.

"The Talmud has a lot about morality, ethics, and such, I gather."

"Yes, that and much more."

"If I put a question in ethics to you, could you give me a Talmudic answer?"

"Are you serious? I'm an utter dilettante."

"So you say. Let's give it a try. It's about this *Challenger* thing."

"I saw your stunt with the ice water on TV."

"Oh, did you?" He chuckles and brightens. "Sneaky, wasn't it?"

He opens up about the commission's report now being compiled. His written views were being kicked around and shunted aside until he threatened to take his name off the report. Then they compromised; his opinions will be published in an appendix.

"They didn't want the Nobel guy pulling out publicly, you see. Not after all the noise about the ice-water business. I've been trouble to them all along. Now the moon man, Neil Armstrong, he belongs on the commission. He's for real, he's an engineer, he knows space. I'm a theorist, a teacher. I was talked into it—patriotic duty and all that—so I did my best, poked around, found things out, and I'm putting in writing what I found. My question's about that appendix." We emerge on the grassy patch at the foot of N Street, where neighborhood dogs are cavorting as usual.

"You see, the President had spoken about sending a teacher into space, and this year, the day the President was to give his State of the Union address, the *Challenger* was launched with a teacher aboard. Coincidence? Most likely, of course, yet two questions still remain unanswered: *Who exactly* gave the word to launch, and why *exactly* did the launch go in dangerously cold weather? The rumors and the hints have been rife, I can tell you. I did some digging and found out quite a bit."

"Anything conclusive?"

"Actually, no."

"Then what's your question?"

"What I did learn runs to a couple of pages. It's the truth, it's not irrelevant, and it's not trivial."

Walking up N Street, we pass a little gray building. "My synagogue. I get up at dawn and learn Talmud here with a friend, for an hour before services."

He squints at it. "Our temple in Far Rockaway was much bigger."

"Orthodox is smaller than Reform. In America, that is."

"Are you honestly Orthodox?" Quizzical note.

"Let me answer your other question first."

Dry laugh. "Shoot."

Long pause as we walk on. Sensitive stuff, that appendix.

"Okay. Talmud aside, here's my opinion, only because you ask for it. What about the families of those astronauts and of that teacher? That's my first thought. Your ice-water moment made you the media star of the commission, more so even than Armstrong. If you, of all people, raise the iffy notion that politics might have influenced the fatal launch, you'll inflict more pain, horrendous pain, on those families. To what purpose? *NASA* bungled the launch. It was NASA, a whole culture, a community of thousands, pressing hard to please the powers that provide the funds. *Who, exactly? Why, exactly?* Those questions stand over. The engineers will learn from the tragedy how to make the shuttles safer. Your appendix will be a strong dose of candor without those pages. Cut them."

"That's brilliant."

"Oh, come on."

"I say 'brilliant,' because it's what I've decided to do myself. Maybe I have a Talmudic mind."

"You'd come by it honestly. You recall that both our fathers were born in Minsk, the Jerusalem of White Russia—this is where I live."

He glances up at the red-brick facades of Smith Row. "Charming. Old."

"Federal, 1815. The university's straight up N Street, another ten minutes or so."

We shake hands. "No answer to my second question?"

"I've written two books on that one. You wouldn't read them."

"No, but why not come along with me and talk? Pleasant here in Georgetown, tree-lined streets, brick sidewalks—"

The Brackets

N Street is mostly uphill from here. He is walking more slowly. "You did the talking in Aspen, and I ate it up," I tell him. "I was learning all the time. Now you're asking me to talk—"

"I've been wondering about some things. You take the Bible seriously?"

"Core of my life."

"Childish fables and all? Creation in six days, Eve and the snake in the garden, Noah's ark, Aaron's stick that turns into a snake, on and on—?"

"How well do you know the Bible?"

"Not well at all. Sorry, what I've glanced at past Genesis has struck me as primitive and boring. In any case, I was turned off all religion in Sunday school when I was ten. For good. As I told you, my father was an atheist. Your father must have been different. We're poles apart."

"We're closer than you think."

"Because we're both Jewish? That's rubbish."

"Have you been to Israel?"

"Not interested. A great physicist, friend of mine, keeps inviting me to come there—"

"You should go."

"Why?"

"Those are the brackets of the Bible story—of our story—Genesis and Israel."

We are at the steep stone staircase to the Georgetown campus. Climbing step by step, he pauses for breath on a landing. "I've been in better shape." On the campus the kids are hurrying to and fro or sitting out on the sunny grass. He makes for a bench and sits down. "Major cancer operation six years ago." He is catching his breath as he speaks. "Damnable waste of limited time, these last three months...So? Talk about the Bible."

"What's our time frame?"

"We're all right."

My paean to the Scripture narratives grabs him, and if I do say so, it should. I know a good deal about narrative. Then I quote gems at random from the wisdom books Proverbs, Ecclesiastes, and of course Job. About Psalms I wax rather lyrical, for me. He is taking it all in, his eyes intensely on me. "The prophets are a whole other treasure house," I wind up, hearing my voice going on too long. "Isaiah, Jeremiah, Amos, and the rest. Much obscure stuff about ancient politics and war, amazing bursts of power and truth. Well, that's the general idea."

"And your point is—if any—that I've missed out on a lot."

"Your father missed out on a lot, like the fathers of most Jews nowadays. Here or in Israel, not that much different. My father grew up in the back room of a Minsk synagogue built of logs, where his father was the sexton and cantor, so I'm the odd man out, not you. I was in my twenties before I began to understand any of this, but for the Jews, modern times have been an exceptionally rough ride—mass move from the old country to the New World, German massacre of those who didn't move, Zionism and the Arab wars to wipe it out—no wonder tradition's been going by the board—"

"Possibly, or possibly it's just become irrelevant."

"So some say. Others like me see it reviving. As for the Bible, the Talmud says it has seventy faces, and the face you've managed to glimpse—an authentic face—is of a hoary epic from Homeric times, but with a big big difference! An *unfinished* epic, running through millennia, continuing today, in which you and I with our brief lives are playing two small parts—you're looking at your watch. I *told* you it took me two books to go into this—"

"You're doing all right. Talk more about the Talmud."

"That's where we're alike, not poles apart. 'Rubbish,' you said? That's dismissive and shallow."

Bristling. "Shallow? Why?"

"Because we are alike. Alike in the joy of following and grasping long strings of tight logic—alike in the zest for the toughest mental challenges, in the rejection of flawed answers, in the glory when the elusive true answer dawns—do you have a Talmudic mind? Sure, call it that, because if you say '*Yiddishe kop,*' Jewish head, you'll enrage the geneticists and get called a racist by fools. Of course it's cultural, it's an inheritance from grandfathers, great-grandfathers, forefathers all the way back to Babylon, and they all studied the Talmud, and that's why you're Feyn-man, I assure you. My pious friends would object that I'm leaving out the main thing, the revelation on Sinai, '*a king-dom of priests, a holy people,*' but never mind. All that is in my books. Right now I'd lose you, and I'd rather not—"

"You wouldn't lose me. I don't believe any of it, that's all, and your comparison is forced and trivial. You know per-fectly well that the glory of an *Aha!* in science comes when long hard experiment confirms a discovery, a new truth of nature. This Talmud glory you speak of comes from figur-ing out old verbal puzzles in old books."

That silences me. A considerable pause.

The Second Question

"Well?" He's having melancholy fun, perhaps, needling me.

"Good shot. You've got me cold with '*old books.*' The Talmud volume on my desk, back in N Street, is from my grandfather's set, and the pages are so yellow that I need strong light to read the print. New editions abound, but I won't use another. I love those crumbling yellow pages, and I love those falling-apart volumes—as I loved the liturgic melodies my father sang around the Bronx flat in my childhood, as I love digging into razor-sharp medieval Bible commentators, as I love the sound of spoken Hebrew in Israel—"

Is there a softening in those hard eyes? "I can understand all that—"

"You can? Well, then, I stand by my comparison. *'Verbal puzzles'* sells the Talmud short. Wordplay, sure—science didn't exist then for those first-class minds to work on—powerful minds in an ongoing game of cut-and-thrust about bedrock issues of human nature and conduct: damage law, property law, ritual law, marital law, criminal law in the terse Mosaic code. The game's immortal. You'd find it rare fun as I do, if you had the tools, which you don't. As I don't have calculus, because I stupidly didn't take your advice and learn the language God talks—"

Amused grunt. "I told you that?"

"In so many words, when we first met at Caltech. Have you read Montaigne? Great French essayist, nobleman, sixteenth century?"

"Some, in college, why?"

"Jewish descent. Spanish forebear burned at the stake. Practicing Catholic, extreme unction on his deathbed. In his essays he gnawed at the edges of disbelief, a risky business then. Too rich and important to get the Galileo treatment, but he was wary, mighty wary. 'I write not as much as I know but as much as I dare, and I dare a little more as I get older.' Well, back in 1959 I dared to write a little book, *This Is My God,* about Judaism. If my grandfather had been alive he would have said, 'Where are you creeping with your lame paws?' It became a sort of popular guide. Forty years later I dared a bit more in a scholarly foray, *The Will to Live On.* Now about your second question—"

"Ah! Here we go—"

"Here we go. Best I can do. To me *Orthodox, Conservative, Reform* are institutional labels rather than bodies of thought. I value every living Jew alike. Our numbers are too frighteningly small to allow anything else. A very few, a sliver of three or four percent, strictly observe the Torah, make it their lifelong study and concern. More power to them, they keep the flame. A sizable few, maybe ten, fifteen percent, try to study and observe while leading busy lives. I guess that's me. The main body of Jewry—*Amkha,* 'Your people'—ranges through all manner of observance, fainter and fainter to no observance, to indifference, to convinced unbelief. I guess that's you, also a lot of the Israel Defense Force, guarding the Land side by side with a lot of believers. Welcome, brother."

A faint smile, a sober nod. "Okay. And how do you handle science and religion? Just shut the conflict from your mind? Compartment it off? Different realms, and so on?"

I point to my watch and laugh. "It's ten to three, have a heart."

"So it is." He makes as if to get up. "This has been interesting."

"Want me to take a ten-minute cut at it?"

Surprised and amused, he settles back. "Why not?"

Deep breath.

"Well, to me they're one realm, not two, but for starters, my handling is Talmudic—"

"I'd like to hear it—"

"Also remember, I'm answering not to convince you of my view, but because you asked me."

Genially, "Granted. Go on."

"Darwin sort of kicked off what you call the conflict. I read every word of *Origin of Species* at sea. It's wonderful. His honesty startled me. He spelled out the gaps he saw in his own theory, based on the science of his day—you've read the book?"

"Some of it, in college. Pretty long, and dense..."

"I know. I had the time at sea to read it through. It wasn't all that controversial when it came out, you know. The first reviews pro and con were respectful. But a storm gathered, all right, and an early lightning bolt was the Huxley-Wilberforce debate. After which—"

"Wait, wait, Huxley I've read. Who's the other guy?"

"Bishop Samuel Wilberforce. At a meeting of a scientific society, their argument over Darwin grew heated— Huxley pro, Wilberforce con—and the bishop threw a sarcastic jab, inquiring whether Huxley thought he was descended from a monkey on his grandfather's or his grandmother's side. Huxley shot back, *"I'd rather be descended from a monkey than a man who misuses great talents to obscure the truth."*

Feynman grins. "Game, set, match."

"Quite, and that crude exchange laid down the battle lines for trench warfare ever since, believers and skeptics volleying arguments over each other's heads. In earlier times, this wasn't so. Religion was moral philosophy, science was natural philosophy, and enlightened men and women could be at home in both. Not today, but your Nobel peer, Steven Weinberg, seems to reach back subtly to that older, broader outlook. In an essay taking an axe to intelligent design, he ends on this civil note: 'It's not that science makes it impossible for intelligent people to be religious—science makes it possible for them *not* to be religious. We should not retreat from this accomplishment—'"

"Weinberg's good."

"So you said when we strolled past an outdoor seminar in Aspen, where he was holding forth."

Wry glance. "You do retain these things."

Counterculture: From Henderson to Wheeler

"Writer's memory. Has John Wheeler ever mentioned Henderson to you?" Feynman looks blank. "Lawrence Henderson, who wrote *Fitness of the Environment*?"

"Oh, yes, the organic chemistry fellow. What about him?"

"You admire Wheeler?"

"John Wheeler? My teacher, my collaborator, my mentor, a very great physicist..."

"Wheeler admires Henderson's book, you know. It came out only fifty years after Darwin's, it's respectful of his theory, doesn't dispute it, just offers a rigid line of logic based on the chemistry of carbon, oxygen, hydrogen, and water, that foreshadows a counterculture in science. This was way back in 1913, and ever since—"

"Hold *on,* now! Counterculture in science? *What* counterculture? In *science?*"

"Counterculture, I say! Cloud no bigger than a man's hand, maybe, but it's there. Henderson was writing not as much as he knew, but as much as he dared. When nearly the whole culture of science was in a froth against Darwin's foes who were holding out for purpose in Nature, Henderson quietly and methodically cited principles of chemistry and experimental data to conclude that in fact the universe was uniquely geared to the existence of life. His term was *biocentric.* You've heard of the anthropic principle?"

"Oho, cat's out of the bag, you've read *that* tome! Weak principle, strong principle, on and on—"

"You've read the book?"

"Glanced at it. Seven hundred pages! No thanks."

"I tried to read it. That march of calculus equations steamrollered me, but the drift was clear: the universe required all these billions of years since the big bang, and all the vastness of space, for an intelligent Observer to emerge into existence—"

"Dreamy speculation—"

"No more? Yet John Wheeler not only admires that book, he ups the ante in *'Genesis and Observership,'* a searching essay he published in Holland, of all places. Was your mentor trying to slip his thought in under the radar, publishing in Holland? He obliquely hints that the universe may require an Observer *to exist at all …*"

"Yes, yes, I know that flight of fancy. It completely loses me—"

"Flight of fancy? Dismissing Wheeler out of hand? The collaborator of Bohr and Einstein who coined the term *black hole,* worked on the atomic bomb, guided you yourself through your doctorate in physics—"

"Look, I'm not putting down John Archibald Wheeler. I revere the man, I love him, but—"

"But these old guys do have their flights of fancy, right? Where do you have to be at three?"

"Medical Center."

"My ten minutes are melting away. Let's go there." We start across the campus in that direction. "Now for my old-guy Talmudic handling of science and religion—"

"I'm all ears."

Teiku

"I've told you that for me they're one realm, not two—also, that you and I are closer than you think. This time hear me out. In the Talmud, when the logic is evenly balanced on both sides, draws close to converging, the Talmud can stop the dispute with one abrupt Aramaic word: *TEIKU!*"

"Tay-ku? Meaning what?"

"Meaning 'the question stands!' Draw, tie, no decision. In Israel today they use *teiku* even about a soccer match. In my yeshiva boyhood, we had a cynical gibe about *teiku*. The prophet Malachi says—they're his last words—'*Behold, I send you the prophet Elijah, before the great and terrible day of the Lord.*' We joked that *teiku* is an acronym for *Tishbi* (Elijah) *will resolve all questions and disputes.* Implied, 'We should live so long! Next subject.' Now, in a TV program you once gave a judgment on religion that's quoted often—"

Amused grunt. "Yes, I know. Too often."

"You don't stand by it?"

"Never saw a reason to change it, though it was just prodded out of me by a nitwit interviewer—"

"Why, it was a beautiful answer, a précis of Psalm 104, pretty near."

"You're laying it on."

"Am I? Look at that psalm sometime. You ad-libbed in clear strong words the enduring wonder of a child. The wonder that powers your science—and powers philosophy, though you despise it, and religion, though you'll have none of it, and all poetry and art—the wonder that even my dulled old heart can feel, looking up above the palm trees into the deep blue desert sky in the dawn. Ecclesiastes put *teiku* another way: *'He has made all things beautiful in their time, and has put eternity in men's hearts, except that no man will find out the work of the Lord from beginning to end.'"*

At the busy R Street entrance to the campus the traffic noise makes Feynman raise his voice, "That is damned good."

"Look, if you ever give the Bible a real shot, Ecclesiastes will become *your* book, believe me. Well, now, you see all those marvels of life on earth and in the cosmos as accidents. Science keeps piling them up as hard facts—as Henderson did in *The Fitness of the Environment*—but no matter how long the odds are getting, *accidents, accidents, accidents!* As yet the counterculture may be an eccentric whisper among the few, but to a believer, the marvels are and always have been God given. One realm, I say! Religion exists in the hearts of men alone, men are short-lived animals, part of Nature—and to believers we are Adam, the creature with a spark of the mind of the Creator—"

The light changes, we walk up R Street, heading toward the Medical Center. "And that's your *teiku?*"

"For this ten-minute ad-lib, yes, that's my *teiku*. The subject's endless, it's been my life since in my twenties my father died, and I found myself facing the dark, a hurt wondering child. It's driven all my storytelling. In your TV statement, you said that in the view of religion all those fantastic marvels exist just so that God can watch men struggle with good and evil, *and 'the stage is too big for the drama'*—forgive me, friend Nobel genius, you're as ignorant of religion as I am of calculus, because you shut out religion for good when you were only ten. Before we part can I ask you something I've often wondered about?"

"Sure. Anything."

"How do you handle sorrow?"

He is no longer beside me. I glance back at him. He stands, looking stricken, even haunted. Silence. Then, hoarsely, "Well, how do *you* handle it?"

"I can't. He helps. And so far as possible, heals."

He looks me in the eye. Short staring contest. The enigmatic smile dawns on that worn Voltairean face. He lightly punches my shoulder. "Almost, I envy you."

At the steep staircase to the Medical Center he holds out his hand. "I've enjoyed myself." We shake hands, he glances at his watch. "Three minutes past three. Well done." Slowly mounting the stairs, he looks back, sees me still there, waves and laughs, "*Teiku!*"

"*Teiku*," I call, and watch until he disappears into the red brick building.

Coda: "Heroes of the *Iliad*"

My book is over. The eternal question stands.

On page 142 I wrote, "Of course I am not Aaron Jastrow, but that [his Theresienstadt sermon] is the nearest I have come, or am ever likely to come, to setting down in words what I believe." First published in 1978 and 1971, respectively, War and Remembrance *and its prologue,* The Winds of War, *have won a place among lovers of literature who relish broad-ranging novels, and also in history courses. For readers of this little book who have not read Jastrow's sermon, here it is in full. He called it "Heroes of the* Iliad" *to throw off the SS. In his own mind he was stating—and stating for me, more or less—the faith of a humanist.*

A large silent audience has gathered, after all. Usually there is lively chatter before the evening's diversion. Not tonight. They have turned out in surprising numbers, but the mood is funereal. Behind the crude lectern, off to a side, stands the curtained puppet theatre. As Natalie takes the vacant seat beside Udam, he gives her a little smile that cuts her heart.

Aaron places his notes on the lectern and looks about, stroking his beard. Softly, in a dry classroom manner, speaking slow formal German, he begins.

"It is interesting that Shakespeare seems to find the whole story of the *Iliad* contemptible. He retells it in his play, *Troilus and Cressida*, and he puts his opinion in the mouth of Thersites, the cynical coward—'*The matter is only a cuckold and a whore.*'"

This quotation Aaron Jastrow cites in English, then with a prudish little smile translates it into German.

"Now Falstaff, that other and more celebrated Shakespearean coward, thinks like Emerson that war in general is nothing but a periodic madness. *'Who hath honor? He that died o' Wednesday.'* We suspect that Shakespeare agreed with his immortal fat man. *Troilus,* his play of the Trojan war, is not in his best tragic vein, for madness is not tragic. Madness is either funny or ghastly, and so is much war literature: either *The Good Soldier Schweik,* or *All Quiet on the Western Front.*

"But the *Iliad* is epic tragedy. It is the same war story as *Troilus,* but with one crucial difference. Shakespeare has taken out the gods, whereas it is the gods who make the *Iliad* grand and terrible.

"For Homer's Hector and Achilles are caught in a squabble of the Greek deities. The gods take sides. They come down into the dust of the battlefield to intervene. They turn aside weapons hurled straight to kill. They appear in disguises to make trouble or to pull their favorites out of jams. An honorable contest of arms becomes a mockery, a game of wits among supernatural, invisible magicians. The fighting men are mere helpless pieces of the game."

Natalie glances over her shoulder at the listeners. No audiences like these! Famished for diversion, for light, for a shred of consolation, they hang on a literary talk in Theresienstadt, as elsewhere people do on a great concert artist's recital, or on a gripping film.

In the same level pedantic way, Jastrow reviews the background of the *Iliad:* Paris's awarding of the golden apple for beauty to Aphrodite; the hostilities on Olympus that ensue; the kidnapping by Paris of Helen, the world's prettiest woman, Aphrodite's promised reward; and the inevitable war, since she is a married Greek queen and he a Trojan prince. Splendid men on both sides, who care nothing for the cuckold, the whore, or the kidnapper, become embroiled. For them, once it is war, honor is at stake.

"But in this squalid quarrel, what gives the heroes of the *Iliad* their grandeur? Is it not their indomitable will to fight, despite the shifting and capricious meddling of the gods? To venture their lives for honor, in an unfair and unfathomable situation where bad and stupid men triumph, good and skilled men fall, and strange accidents divert and decide battles? In a purposeless, unfair, absurd battle, to fight on, fight to the death, fight like men? It is the oldest of human problems, the problem of senseless evil, dramatized on the field of battle. That is the tragedy Homer perceived and Shakespeare passed over."

Jastrow pauses, turns a page, and looks straight at the audience, his emaciated face dead pale, his eyes large in the sunken sockets. If the audience has been silent before, it is now as quiet as so many corpses.

"The universe of the *Iliad,* in short, is a childish and despicable trap. The glory of Hector is that in such a trap he behaves so nobly that an Almighty God, if He did exist, would weep with pride and pity. Pride, that He has created out of a handful of dirt a being so grand. Pity, that in His botched universe a Hector must unjustly die, and his poor corpse be dragged in the dust. But Homer knows no Almighty God. There is Zeus, the father of the gods, but who can say what he is up to? Perhaps he is off mounting some bemused mortal girl in the disguise of her husband, or a bull, or a swan. Small wonder that Greek mythology is extinct."

The disgusted gesture with which Jastrow turns his page surprises an uncertain laugh from the rapt audience. Thrusting his notes into his pocket, Jastrow leaves the lectern, comes forward, and stares at his listeners. His usually placid face is working. He bursts out in another voice, startling Natalie by shifting to Yiddish, in which he has never lectured before.

"All right. Now let us talk about this in our mother language. And let us talk about an epic of our own. Satan says to God, you remember, 'Naturally Job is upright. Seven sons, three daughters, the wealthiest man in the land of Uz. Why not be upright? Look how it pays. A sensible universe! A fine arrangement! Job is not upright, he is just a smart Jew. The sinners are damned fools. But just take away his rewards, and see how upright he will remain!'

"'All right, take them away,' God says. And in one day marauders carry off Job's wealth, and a hurricane kills all his ten children. What does Job do? He goes into mourning. 'Naked I came from the womb, naked I will return,' he says, 'God has given, God has taken away. Blessed be God's name.'

"So God challenges Satan. 'See? He remained upright. A good man.'

"'Skin for skin,' Satan answers. 'All a man really cares about is his life. Reduce him to a skeleton—a sick, plundered, bereaved skeleton, nothing left to this proud Jew but his own rotting skin and bones—'"

Jastrow loses his voice. He shakes his head, clears his throat, passes a hand over his eyes. He goes on hoarsely. "God says, 'All right, do anything to him except kill him.' A horrible sickness strikes Job. Too loathsome an object to stay under his own roof, he crawls out and sits on an ash heap, scraping his sores with a shard. He says nothing. Stripped of his wealth, his children senselessly killed, his body a horrible stinking skeleton covered with boils, he is silent. Three of his pious friends come to comfort him. A debate follows.

"Oh, my friends, what a debate! What rugged poetry, what insight into the human condition! I say to you that Homer pales before Job; that Aeschylus meets his match in power, and his master in understanding; that Dante and Milton sit at this author's feet without ever grasping him. Who was he? Nobody knows. Some old Jew. He knew what life is, that's all. He knew it as we in Theresienstadt know it."

He pauses, looking straight at his niece with sad eyes. Shaken, perplexed, on the verge of tears, Natalie is hungry for his next words. When he speaks, though he looks away, she feels he is talking to her.

"In Job, as in most great works of art, the main design is very simple. His comforters maintain that since one Almighty God rules the universe, it must make sense. Therefore Job must have sinned. Let him search his deeds, confess and repent. The missing piece is only what his offense was.

"And in round after round of soaring argument, Job fights back. The missing piece must be with God, not with him. He is as religious as they are. He knows that the Almighty exists, that the universe must make sense. But he, poor bereft boil-covered skeleton, knows now that it does not in fact always make sense;

that there is no guarantee of good fortune for good behavior; that crazy injustice is part of the visible world, and of his life. His religion demands that he assert his innocence, *otherwise he will be profaning God's name!* He will be conceding that the Almighty can botch one man's life; and if God can do that, the whole universe is a botch, and He is not an Almighty God. That Job will never concede. He wants an answer.

"He gets an answer! Oh, what an answer! An answer that answers nothing. God Himself speaks at last out of a roaring storm. '*Who are you to call me to account? Can you hope to understand why or how I do anything? Were you there at the Creation? Can you comprehend the marvels of the stars, the animals, the infinite wonders of existence? You, a worm that lives a few moments, and dies?'*

"My friends, Job has won! Do you understand? God with all his roaring has *conceded Job's main point, that the missing piece is with Him!* God claims only that His reason is beyond Job. That, Job is perfectly willing to admit. With the main point settled, Job humbles himself, is more than satisfied, falls on his face.

"So the drama ends. God rebukes the comforters for speaking falsely of Him, and praises Job for holding to the truth. He restores Job's wealth. Job has seven more sons and three more daughters. He lives a hundred and forty more years, sees grandchildren and great-grandchildren, and dies old, prosperous, revered."

The rich flow of literary Yiddish halts. Jastrow goes back to the lectern, pulls the notes from his pocket, and turns over several sheets. He peers out at the audience.

"Satisfied? A happy ending, yes? Much more Jewish than the absurd and tragic *Iliad*?

"Are you so sure? My dear Jewish friends, what about the ten children who died? Where was God's justice to them? And what about the father, the mother? Can those scars on Job's heart heal, even in a hundred and forty years?

"That is not the worst of it. Think! What was the missing piece that was too much for Job to understand? *We* understand it, and are we so very clever? Satan simply sneered God into ordering the senseless ordeal. No wonder God roars out of a storm to silence Job! Isn't He ashamed of Himself before His own creature? Hasn't Job behaved better than God?"

Jastrow shrugs, spreads his hands, and his face relaxes in a wistful little smile that makes Natalie think of Charlie Chaplin.

"But I am expounding the *Iliad*. In the *Iliad,* unseen powers are at odds with each other, and that brings about a visible world of senseless evil. Not so in Job. Satan has no power at all. He is not the Christian Satan, not Dante's colossal monster, not Milton's proud rebel, not in the least. He needs God's permission to make every move.

"Then who is Satan, and why does God leave him out of the answer in the storm? The word *satan* in Hebrew means *adversary*. What is the book telling us? Was God arguing with Himself? Was He asking Himself whether there was any purpose in the vast creation? And in reply pointing, not to the dead glittering galaxies that sprawl over thousands of light-years, but to man, the handful of dirt that can sense His presence, do His will, and measure those galaxies? Above all, to the upright man, the speck of dirt who can measure himself against the Creator Himself, for dignity and goodness? What else did the ordeal establish?

"The heroes in the *Iliad* rise superior to the squabbling injustice of weak and contemptible gods.

"The hero in Job holds to the One Almighty God through the most senseless and horrible injustice; forcing God at last to measure up to Himself, to acknowledge that injustice is on His side, to repair the damage as best He can.

"In the *Iliad* there is no injustice to repair. In the end there is only blind fate.

"In Job God must answer for everything, good and bad, that happens. Job is the Bible's only hero. There are fighting men, patriarchs, lawgivers, prophets in the other books. This is the one man who rises to the measure of the universe, to the stature of the God of Israel, while sitting on an ash heap; Job, a poor skeletal broken beggar.

"Who is Job?

"Nobody. *'Job was never born and never existed,'* says the Talmud. *'He was a parable.'*

"Parable of what truth?

"All right, we have come to it now. Who is it in history who will never admit that there is no God, never admit that the universe makes no sense? Who is it who suffers ordeal after ordeal, plundering after plundering, massacre after massacre, century after century, yet looks up at the sky, sometimes with dying eyes, and cries, 'The Lord our God, the Lord is One'?

"Who is it who in the end of days will force from God the answer from the storm? Who will see the false comforters rebuked, the old glory restored, and generations of happy children and grandchildren to the fourth generation? Who until then will leave the missing piece to God, and praise His Name, crying, 'The Lord has given, the Lord has taken away, blessed be the Name of the Lord'? Not the noble Greek of the *Iliad*, he is extinct. No! Nobody but the sick, plundered skeleton on the ash heap. Nobody but the beloved of God, the worm that lives a few moments and dies, the handful of dirt that has justified Creation. Nobody but Job. He is the only answer, if there is one, to the adversary challenge to an Almighty God, if there is One. Job, the stinking Jew."

Jastrow stares in a stunned way at the still audience, then stumbles toward the first row. Udam jumps up and gently helps him to his seat. The audience does not applaud, does not talk, does not move.

Udam begins to sing.

Udam...udam...udam...

So there will be no puppet show. Natalie joins in the chorusing of the tragic refrain. Udam sings his song for the last time in Theresienstadt, driving it to a heartrending crescendo.

When it ends, there is no reaction. No applause, no talk, nothing. This silent audience is waiting for something.

Udam does something he has never done before; an encore; an encore to no applause. He starts another song, one Natalie has heard in Zionist meetings. It is an old simple syncopated refrain, in a minor key, built on a line from the liturgy: *"Let the temple be rebuilt, soon in our time, and grant us a portion in your Law."* As he sings it, Udam slowly begins to dance.

Sheh-yi-boneh bet-hamikdash
Bim-hera b'yomenu—

He dances as an old rabbi might on a holy day, deliberately, awkwardly, his arms raised, his face turned upward, his eyes closed, his fingers snapping the rhythm. The people softly accompany him, singing and clapping their hands. One by one they rise to their feet. Udam's voice grows more powerful, his steps more vigorous. He is losing himself in the dance and the song, drifting into an ecstasy terrible and beautiful to see. Barely opening his eyes, twisting and swaying, he moves toward Aaron Jastrow, and holds out a hand. Jastrow gets to his feet, links his hand with Udam's, and the two men dance and sing.

It is a death dance. Natalie knows it. Everybody knows it. The sight both freezes and exalts her. It is the most stirring moment of her life, here in this dark malodorous loft in a prison ghetto. She is overwhelmed with the agony of her predicament, and the exaltation of being Jewish.

About the Author

Herman Wouk is best known for the linked monumental books, The Winds of War *(1971) and* War and Remembrance *(1978), which were both number one bestsellers and remained on the* New York Times *list for over a year. Of his earlier works,* The Caine Mutiny *(1951) won the Pulitzer Prize, and* Marjorie Morningstar *followed, the most widely read American novel of 1955.* The Language God Talks *retraces much of Wouk's own life: birth in the Bronx to Russian immigrant parents, Columbia education, early radio comedy writing, years in the wartime Pacific as a reserve naval officer, and renowned novelist. In the Judaic field Wouk has written* This Is My God *(1959), a popular guide to the faith, and* The Will to Live On *(2001). Among his plays,* The Caine Mutiny Court-Martial *is an ongoing international success.*

The papers and manuscripts of The Winds of War, War and Remembrance, *and his subsequent works—including the memoir-novel* Inside, Outside, *his own favorite among his* books—can now be found at the Library of Congress. The library of Columbia University has the archive of his earlier works, among them City Boy, Youngblood Hawke, and Don't Stop the Carnival. The author's many honors include honorary degrees from the Hebrew University of Jerusalem and Bar-Ilan University in Beersheba.

His wife of sixty-four years, Betty Sarah, acts as his editor and literary agent. They have lived in New York, the Virgin Islands, Washington, DC, and Israel. They currently live in Palm Springs, California, where he is writing a new book.